Crochet WORK

Adapted from *The Encyclopedia of Needlework*

Crochet WORK

Learn Crochet Work Step-by-Step

Thérèse de Dillmont

Plain Sight Publishing
An Imprint of Cedar Fort, Inc.
Springville, Utah

The original *Encyclopedia of Needlework* by Thérèse de Dillmont was published in 1886. It has since been translated into at least 17 languages and published again and again over the last century. The complete work boasts over 600 pages of detailed explanations regarding the delicate craft of needlework. While the comprehensive work is valuable indeed, making specific chapters available that focus on one craft in particular seemed like a convenient alternative. This book is the result of that thought.

*Note: The preface on page ix is from the original, complete book but is being included in this version of the shortened book anyway.

Published by Plain Sight Publishing, an imprint of Cedar Fort, Inc.
2373 W. 700 S., Springville, UT 84663
Distributed by Cedar Fort, Inc., www.cedarfort.com

LIBRARY OF CONGRESS CATALOGING-IN-PUBLICATION DATA

Dillmont, Thérèse de, 1846-1890, author.
Crochet work / Thérèse de Dillmont.
pages cm
Originally published in 1886 as a chapter in the Encyclopedia of Needlework.
ISBN 978-1-4621-1186-2 (alk. paper)
1. Crocheting. I. Title.

TT820.D49 2013
746.43'4--dc23

2012050327

Cover, page design, and typesetting by Angela D. Olsen

Printed in the United States of America

10 9 8 7 6 5 4 3 2 1

Have you ever wished you could locate a book that included precise details on how to do all types of needlework? One that wouldn't be so massive that it would be hard to tote around or store? It's here finally in the revised paperback edition of *The Complete Encyclopedia of Needlework* by Thérèse de Dillmont.

—*Chicago Sun Times*

Excellent book. Every library as well as every art teacher in junior high and high school should have it. It has been valuable in French for years.

—*Library Materials Guide*, National Union of Christian Schools.

This enormous compendium . . . dates back to the 19th century and is still a basic reference work in it's field; the hyperbolic-seeming title is, in reality, a sober, factual description of its scope.

—*Washington Post Book World*

Contents

CONTENTS

Preface

The absolute want of any comprehensive book on needlework—one that contains both written and pictorial descriptions of everything included under the name of needlework—has led me to create an encyclopedia, all the knowledge and experience, which years of unceasing study and practice have enabled me to accumulate on the subject, with the hope that diligent female workers of all ages may be able to teach themselves in every branch of slip and fancy needlework.

All of the patterns given, even the most insignificant, were worked afresh for this book to make sure that the explanations and representations are accurate and intelligible.

In order to provide my readers with something besides dull theory, this work is enlivened by a number of useful patterns, some new, some derived from the artistic productions of such countries and epochs as have become famous by special excellence in the domain of needlework.

Though at first sight, the reproduction of many of these patterns may seem to present difficulties, they will, after a careful study of the text, and exact attention to the directions given, prove easy to carry out.

Many of these interesting designs are drawn from private collections, whose owners, with great kindness, placed their treasures at my disposal, to copy and borrow from at discretion, for which I desire to take the present opportunity, of tendering them my warmest thanks.

My readers will find the choice of colors and material—a difficult matter to many—rendered comparatively easy to them by the notes affixed to the illustrations; and I may point out that most of the patterns were worked with DMC cottons, which enjoy the well-earned reputation of being, the very best of their kind in the market of the world.

Experience has convinced me that, in many instances, these cottons may with advantage take the place of wool, linen thread, and even silk.

If this work is well accepted, and proves really useful, I shall find ample reward in that fact for the trouble and difficulties that have unavoidably attended its completion.

Crochet lace.—Close leaves and bars with picots

Crochet Work

Crochet work, so called from the hook, French *croche* or *croc*, with which it is done, is not only one of the easiest but in comparison with the cost and labor, one of the most effective kinds of fancy-work. It is also one of the most useful, as it can be applied to the domestic requirements of everyday life, to wearing apparel, house-linen, and upholstery. We are sure that the patterns contained in this chapter, which have in addition to their other merits that of novelty, will favorably received.

Hooks, or needles as they are generally called, made of wood, bone, or tortoiseshell are used for all the heavier kinds of crochet work involving thick wool or cotton, and steel ones for the finer work. The Tunisian crochet is done with a long straight hook, which is made of one piece. The points should be well polished inside and not too sharp, with the backs slightly curved, and the handles, whether of bone, steel or wood, so light as not to tire the hand. We consider those hooks represented here to have the best shape. As it is most essential that the needle should be suited to the cotton in size, we include a comparative table of the numbers of the DMC threads and cottons and of the different needles.

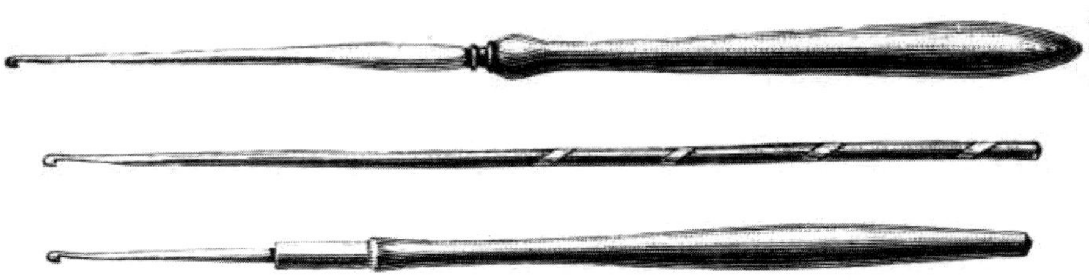

Table of the approximate relation of the D.M.C threads and cottons to the numbers of the crochet needles.

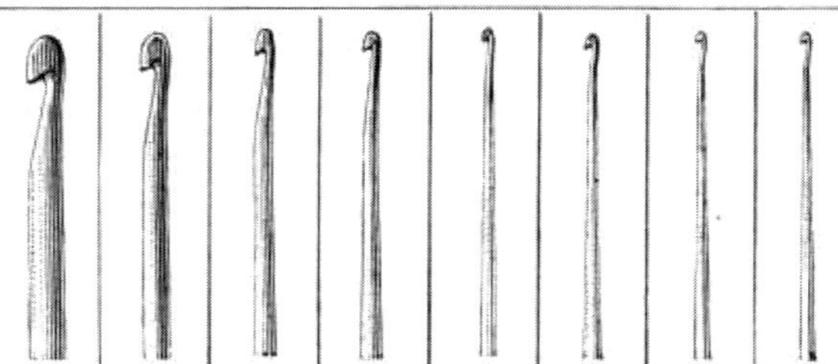

Numbers of the crochet needles.	9	10	11	12	13	14	16	18
Numbers of the cottons	No.	No.	No.	No.	No.	No.	No.	No.
Coton pour crochet....	—	6	8—10	12—14	16—20	24—40	—	—
Coton à tricoter.......	6	8	10—12	14—16	18—25	25—40	50	—
Fil à pointer..........	10	15	20—30	—	—	—	—	—
Cordonnet 6 fils.......	1—1½	2—2½	3—4	10—15	20—30	40—60	70—90	100—150
Fil d'Alsace...........	—	—	—	—	30	36—50	60—90	100—150
Fil à dentelle.........	—	—	—	—	25	30—50	60—90	100—150

Table of the approximate relation of the DMC threads and cottons to the numbers of the crochet needles.

Explanation of the symbols *.—In crochet, as in knitting, you frequently have to repeat the same series of stitches. Such repetitions will be indicated by the signs *, **, ***, etc., as the case may be.

Crochet stitches.—In point of fact, there is only one stitch, because all crochet work consists of loops made by means of the hook or needle and connected together by being drawn one through the other.

Crochet work may, however, be divided into two kinds: German crochet and Victoria or Tunisian crochet; the latter is known also under the name of *tricot-crochet*.

In German crochet, there are eight different kinds of stitches: (1) chain stitch, (2) single stitch, (3) slip stitch, (4) double crochet stitch, (5) knot stitch, (6) bullion stitch, (7) cluster or scale stitch, and (8) double stitch.

The rows are worked, according to the kind of stitch, either back and forth or all from one end. In the former case, the work has to be turned at the end of each row, and the subsequent row begun with 1, 2, or 3 chain stitches to prevent the contraction of the outside edge.

When the rows are all worked one way, the thread must be fastened on each time, which is done by putting the needle into the first chain stitch of the preceding row, drawing the thread through it so as to form a loop, and making one or more chain stitches according to the height required.

At the end of each row, cut the thread and draw the end through the last loop; in this manner all crochet work is finished off. Some crochet workers make a few extra chain stitches with the ends of the thread at the beginning and end of each row, or fasten them off with a few stitches on the wrong side.

The stitches can also, when the occasion requires, be formed into a fringe or tassels as a finish to the work.

Position of the hands and explanation of (1) **chain stitch** (Fig. 403).—Take the thread in the left hand between the first finger and thumb, hold the needle between the thumb and first finger of the right hand, letting it rest on the second finger, in the same manner in which you hold your pen, and put it into the loop, which you hold between the finger and thumb of the left hand. Take up the thread, lying on your finger, with the needle and make your first stitch as you do in knitting, tightening the loop just enough to leave an easy passage through it for the needle. The end of the thread must be held by the thumb and forefinger. The next stitches are made by taking up the thread with the needle and drawing it through the loop. The throwing of the thread round the needle by a jerk of the wrist is called an "over."

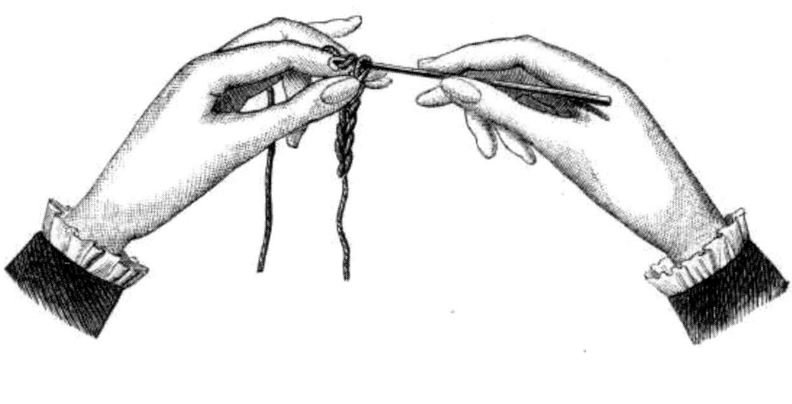

Figure 404

Single stitch

(Fig. 404).—Put the needle in from the right side of the work, into the uppermost loop of the preceding row, then take up the thread on the needle and draw it through both loops.

Figure 405

Slip stitch

(Fig. 405).—Put the needle through, as in fig. 404, from the right side to the wrong, under the upper side, either of a chain, or of a stitch of the preceding row. Draw the thread through it in a loop, turn the thread round the needle, and draw it through both loops on the needle. By making the rows of slip stitches follow each other in different ways, a great variety of stitches can be produced, as the illustrations and written instructions given here will show.

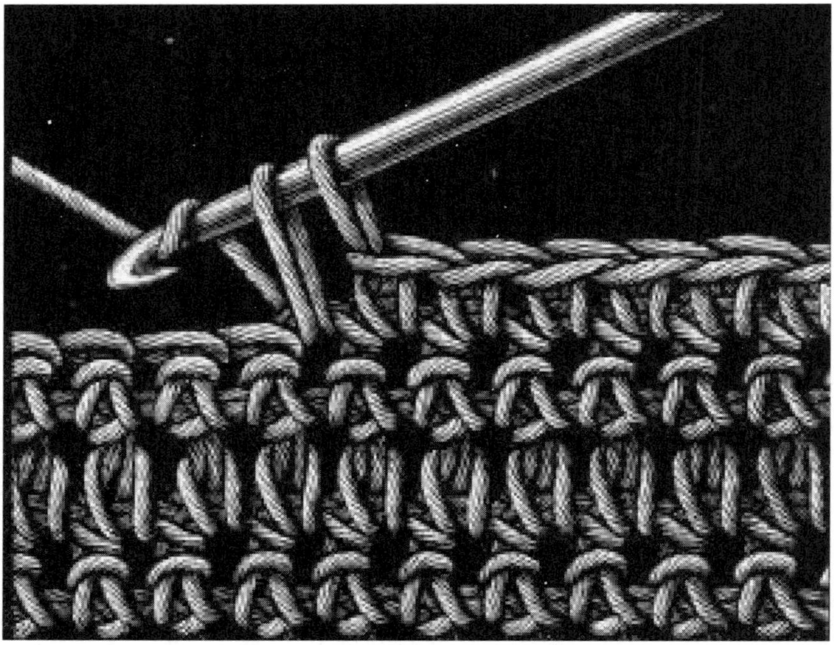

Figure 406

Rose stitch

(Fig. 406).—This consists of rows of slip stitches worked backward and forward. Insert the needle from the right side, under both the horizontal loops of the preceding row.

Figure 407

Russian stitch

(Fig. 407).—This is worked like the rose stitch, except that all the rows have to be begun from the same end, and the thread has to be cut off at the end of each row.

Figure 408

Ribbed stitch

(Fig. 408).—This is worked backward and forward, the hook being passed through the back part only of the stitches of the preceding row.

Chain stitch

Worked like fig. 408, but on one side only.

Piqué stitch

This stitch is also only worked on one side. Put the needle in under one of the vertical threads of a stitch and complete the slip stitch. This is a stitch that looks very good on the wrong side; the bars of the loop lie quite close together, which makes it particularly suitable for unlined articles of clothing. A large-sized needle is required to do this stitch well, especially if the material is heavy.

Figure 409

Slanting stitch

(Fig. 409).—This stitch is worked entirely on the right side. Take up the back thread of a stitch in the preceding row, take hold of the crochet thread without turning it round the needle, and draw it through in a loop, then finish the stitch like a slip stitch.

Crossed-double stitch

This is the same as the preceding stitch, except that both the threads of the stitches in the row before are taken up together, instead of the back one only.

Figure 410

Russian crossed stitch

(Fig. 410).—This stitch runs in slanting lines. To work it, put the needle in between the vertical threads of the stitches and underneath the two horizontal ones.

Figure 411

Counterpane stitch

(Fig. 411).—Counterpanes can be made with a less close stitch than those just described.

To produce a soft and elastic fabric, turn the thread round the needle and insert it under both the horizontal threads of a loop, take up the thread without turning it round the needle, draw it through in a loop, make an over, and draw the thread through all the three loops that you have on the needle.

Figure 412

Knotted stitch

(Fig. 412).—This stitch likewise is composed of slip stitches, which, however differ in slightly from those we have previously described.

Make an over, put the needle through the two horizontal threads of the stitch below, make another over and draw it back through the two loops and the first over, make another over, and draw the thread through the last two loops.

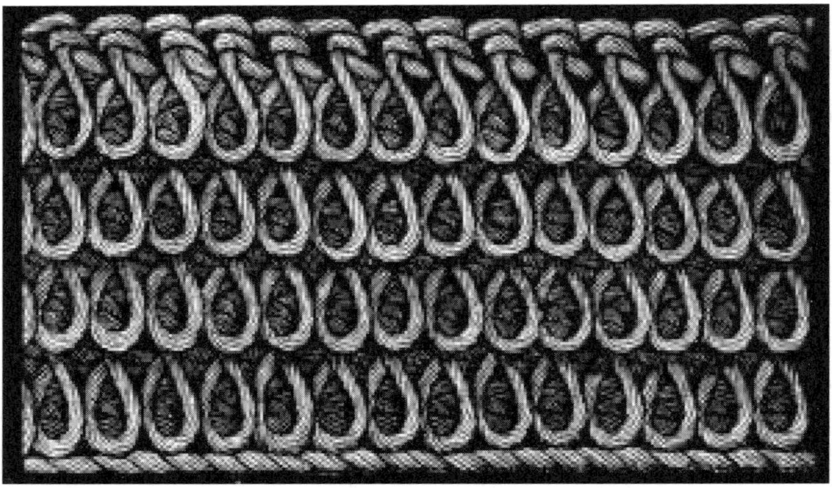

Figure 413

Loop stitch

(Fig. 413).—When you have put the needle into the loop of a stitch below, carry the thread, downward from above, round a stripe of cardboard or a flat wooden ruler, then finish the stitch in the usual way. These long loops, each about 2 cm (¾ in.) in length, can also be made over the forefinger and held fast by the thumb as you work, but it is more difficult to make them regular in this way.

Each row of long stitches is followed by a row of slip stitches. The side, where the long loops lie becomes the right side. If you wish this stitch to be very thick and attractive, wind the thread three times round the ruler or finger, and secure it with a slip stitch; in this case, you should make one slip stitch between every two clusters. A loose, fleecy thread is generally used for this stitch, and for washing articles more especially, we recommend Coton à repriser DMC.

Figure 414

Slip stitches for a chain

(Fig. 414).—Begin with two chain stitches. Put the needle in between the two threads of the first chain stitch, turn the thread round the needle, and draw it through in a loop. Turn it round again and draw it through the two loops; then, put the needle into the left part of the stitch that was just made, turn the thread round the needle, draw it through the two loops and so on, to the end.

A chain of this kind makes a very good substitute for *mignardise* when that cannot be got of the right size and color for the required purpose.

Figure 416

Figure 417

Double crochet

Double crochet are little columns, or bars, made of loops or stitches. (They can be worked like all other crochet, either back and forth, or all one way.) There are different kinds of double crochet: half or short double crochet, double crochet, trebles (also called the "long stitch"), double and tripe trebles (called the "extra long stitch"), connected double crochet, and crossed double crochet. (Figs. 416 and 417).—Begin, as for the half double crochet, by wrapping the thread round the needle and putting it in under one edge of the stitch beneath. Then take up the thread on the needle and bring it through two of the loops, take it up again, and draw it through the two remaining loops.

In fig. 417, we have double crochet made in the same manner as fig. 416, except that instead of putting the needle under one edge of the stitch beneath, you put it under both, and between the double crochets of the last row.

Figure 415

Half double crochet

(Fig. 415).—Wrap the thread round the needle from behind; put the needle in between the double crochets of the preceding row, or into one edge of a chain stitch; make an over, bring the needle forward again with the thread, make another over and draw the needle through all three loops.

Figure 418

Trebles or "long stitch"

(Fig. 418).—Turn the thread twice round the needle, put it into a stitch of the work, and bring the thread through in a loop, then take up the thread on the needle and bring it through two of the loops, three times in succession.

Figure 419

Double and triple trebles or "extra long stitches"

(Fig. 419).—For a double treble, wrap the cotton three times round the needle, or four times for a quadruple one, then form the double crochet in the usual way by bringing the needle through two of the loops at a time. To make a series of double crochets of gradually increasing length, bring the needle, at every other treble, through the last three loops, so that before making a double treble, you will have to make columns, respectively, 1 treble, 1½ treble, 2 double crochets and 2½ double crochets long. Columns like these, of different lengths, are often required in crochet work for leaves and scalloped edgings.

Figure 420

Connected double crochet

(Fig. 420).—Double crochets, connected together, can be worked back and forth, and take the place of slip stitches. Begin with a chain, then make a double crochet of the required height. Form as many loops as you made overs for the treble, take up the upper thread of the stitch nearest the treble, turn the thread round the needle, bring it back to the right side, and draw the needle through the double crochets, two at a time.

Figure 421

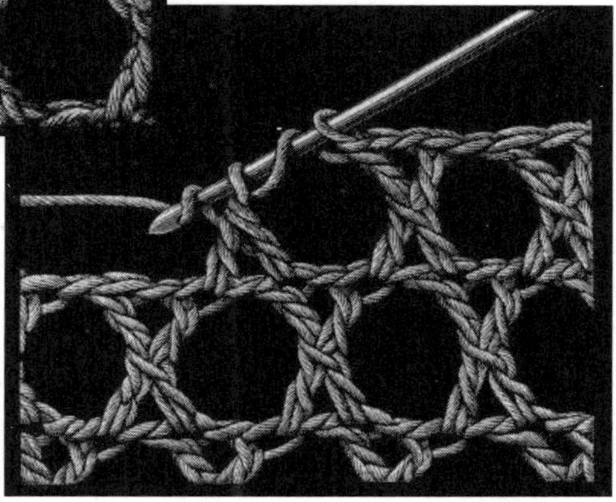

Figure 422

Crossed double crochet

(Figs. 421 and 422).—Double crochets of this sort produce an open stitch, which is often used for the footing of lace or for an insertion. Make a foundation chain, or other stitches, and proceed as follows: chain 3, skip 2 stitches of the row beneath, make 1 double crochet in the third stitch, chain 5, 1 over, put the needle in between the loops of the connected double crochets, and finish with a treble. Then make a double over, put the needle into the next loop of the preceding row, make another over, draw the needle through the loops, make another over, and join the next two loops. This leaves 3 loops on the needle. Make an over, put the needle into the third stitch of the row beneath, make an over, and bring the needle back to the right side.

Join the 5 loops on the needle together, 2 and 2, chain 2, 1 over, put the needle into the upper parts of the connected double crochets, finish with a treble, and so on.

These double crochets also can be lengthened if necessary, but in that case, the width of the crossed double crochet must correspond with the height. Generally speaking, you make the double crochets over the same number of stitches as you made overs on the needle, which should always be an even number. Fig. 422. Crossed double crochets are set between those of the preceding row.

Double crochets for a chain

—A quicker way of making a wide footing for a crochet lace is to make the double crochets in the following manner.

Make 4 chain stitches, 2 overs, put the needle into the first of the 4 chain, 1 over, draw the thread through the stitch *, 1 over, draw the thread through the next 2 loops and repeat twice from * = ** 2 overs, put the needle into the left bottom part of the treble, close the double crochet as before, and repeat from **.

Figure 423

Knot stitch

(Fig. 423).—This stitch, which is composed of several loops forming a tuft, can only be worked from one side, and consequently must be worked all one way. It looks best in a coarse material, which shows off the interlacing of the threads.

Enter the needle through the two loops of the stitches of the bottom row, turn the thread round the needle, but away from you, toward the back; bring it forward to the right side, put the needle again through one of the bottom stitches, make another over like the first, and draw the needle through all the bars at once.

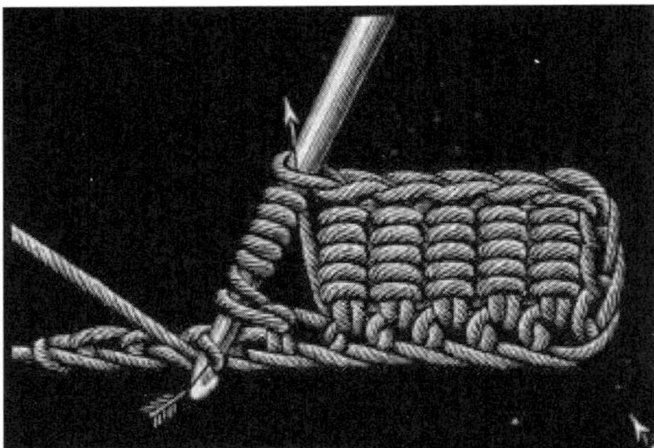

Figure 424

Figure 425

Bullion stitch

(Figs. 424 and 425).—For a bullion stitch, select a needle a little thicker toward the handle and finer at the tip than you would use for any other crochet stitch.

Begin by making a chain of very loose stitches, then wind the thread several times, very evenly, round the needle. Insert the needle into a loop of the chain, make a single over, and draw it with the last over upon it, through all the other overs.

Double crochets in bullion stitch (as shown in fig. 425), are worked in just the same manner, except that you have to wind the thread at least 10 or 12 times round the needle and draw it through all the overs at once. To facilitate the passage of the needle, keep the overs in their place with the thumb and forefinger of the left hand.

The bullion stitch can only be worked with wool or a very fleecy thread, such as Coton à repriser DMC, [A], but double crochets in bullion stitch can be worked in any of the DMC threads and cottons.

Figure 426

Cluster stitch

(Fig. 426).—This is generally used as an insertion between rows of slip crochet.

Put the needle under one stitch of the preceding row, make an over, draw the thread through in a loop, make another over, put the needle in again under the same stitch, bring it back, make a third over, and pass a third time under the same stitch; bring the needle back, make a fourth over and pass the needle through all the loops that are upon it.

Then, after making a chain stitch, begin the same stitch over again, placing it in the second stitch of the lower row.

A cluster stitch may also be finished off by retaining the two last loops on the needle, making an over, and ending with a slip stitch.

Figure 427

Double stitch

(Fig. 427).—A rather coarse thread, such as Coton à tricoter DMC Nos. 6 to 12, Cordonnet 6 fils DMC Nos. 3 to 10, or Fil à pointer DMC Nos. 10 to 30[A] is better for this stitch than a loose fleecy thread, which is apt to render it indistinct. Take up a loop right and left of a stitch of the preceding row, so that, counting the loop of the last stitch, you have 3 loops on the needle. Make an over and draw it through the 3 loops. Then take up a loop again by the side of the one you made on the left, which now lies on the right. Take 2 loops in the next stitch, make an over and draw it through all the loops.

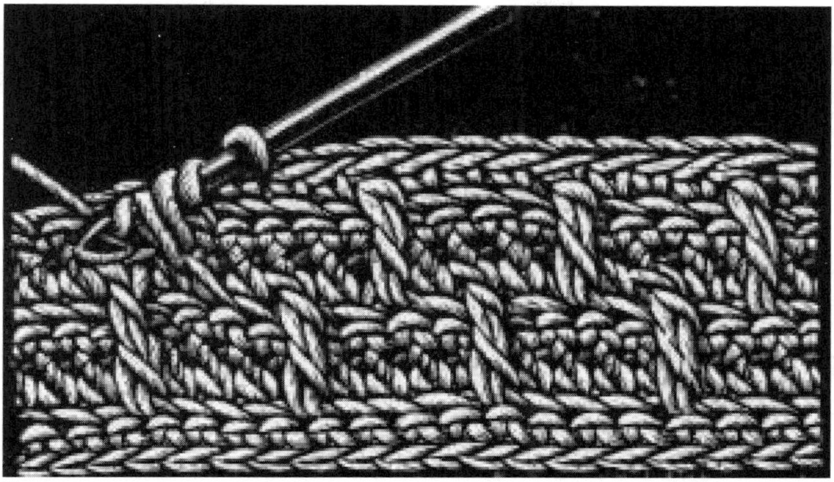

Figure 428

Raised stitch

(Fig. 428).—All the stitches that come under this heading require a foundation of a few slip rows for the raised double crochets. In fig. 428, you will observe that the fourth stitch in the fourth row is a treble, connected with a loop of the fourth stitch of the first row.

Skip the stitch of the preceding row, which is hidden under the treble, make 3 slip stitches, 1 treble, and so on.

Having finished this row, turn the work and make a slip row. In the next row begin with 4 slip stitches, then make 1 treble between the 3 stitches that are between the first double crochets, 3 slip stitches, 2 trebles, and so on.

In the 8th row of slip stitches, the double crochets must be placed in the same order as in the 4th.

Figure 429

Raised stitch with crossed double crochet

(Fig. 429).—Begin, as in fig. 428, with 3 rows of slip stitches. The 4th row begins with 2 slip stitches followed by * 1 treble joined to the upper part of the 1st stitch of the 1st row; keep the 2 last loops of this double crochet on the needle; make a double over for the next treble; pass the needle through the fourth stitch of the first row. Make an over, turn the thread round the needle, bring it back, finish the double crochet all but the last 3 loops of the treble, which you crochet together. Skip the stitch behind the treble, make 3 slip stitches, and repeat from *.

Then turn the work, make one slip row, and turn the work back to the right side.

The second row of double crochets begins with a slip stitch. The way in which the double crochets are to be crossed is shewn in the illustration.

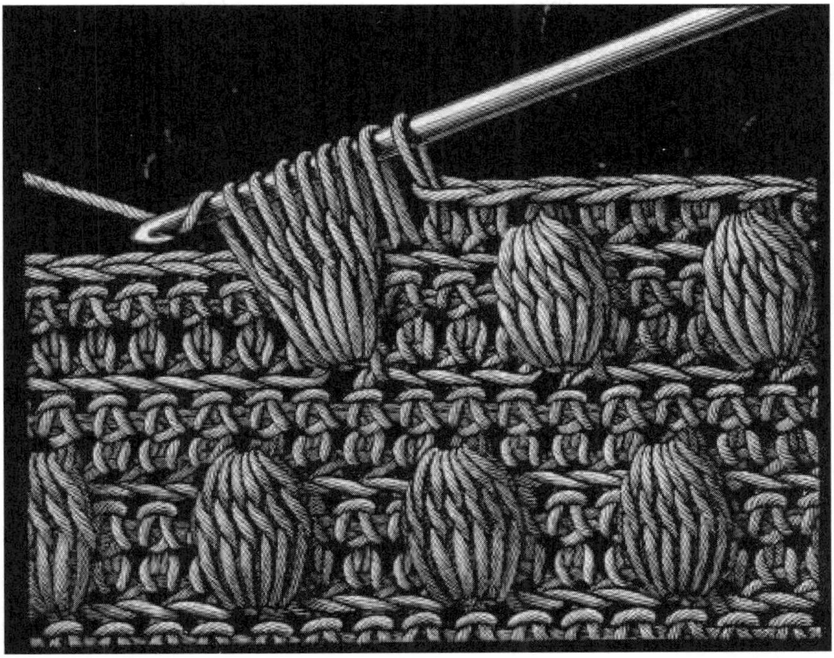

Figure 430

Raised stitch with dots

(Fig. 430).—After making 3 slip rows, begin the 4th with 3 slip stitches, and proceed as follows: * make 6 double crochets into the 4th slip stitch of the preceding row, leaving the last loop of each double crochet on the needle, so that altogether you have 7 loops upon it; then turn the thread once round the needle and draw it through the loops; skip the stitch that is underneath the dot, make 3 slip stitches, and repeat from *.

Then make 3 rows of slip stitches; in the 4th row, the 1st dot is made in the 4th stitch, so that the dots stand out in relief.

Figure 431

Raised dots with double crochet

(Fig. 431).—Make 3 rows of slip stitches and turn the work. Make 3 more stitches more in the 4th stitch of the 1st row, * make 6 double crochets, drop the last stitch of the 6th treble, put the needle into the stitch between the last slip stitch and the 1st treble, and take the dropped loop of the last double crochet and draw it through the one on the needle; skip the stitch under the dot, make 5 slip stitches, and repeat from *.

Figure 432

Raised dots in slanting lines

(Fig. 432).—On the rows of stitches that have been previously prepared, make a cluster stitch for the 4th stitch of the 4th row, as in fig. 426, with 1 quadruple over and then 4 slip stitches, 1 cluster stitch and so on. The next row is slip. In the second you have to make 1 slip stitch more and fasten the cluster stitches into the loops to the left of the second of the 3 covered rows. In this way you have to make each raised stitch one stitch in advance and to the left of the last, so that they run in slanting lines over the surface.

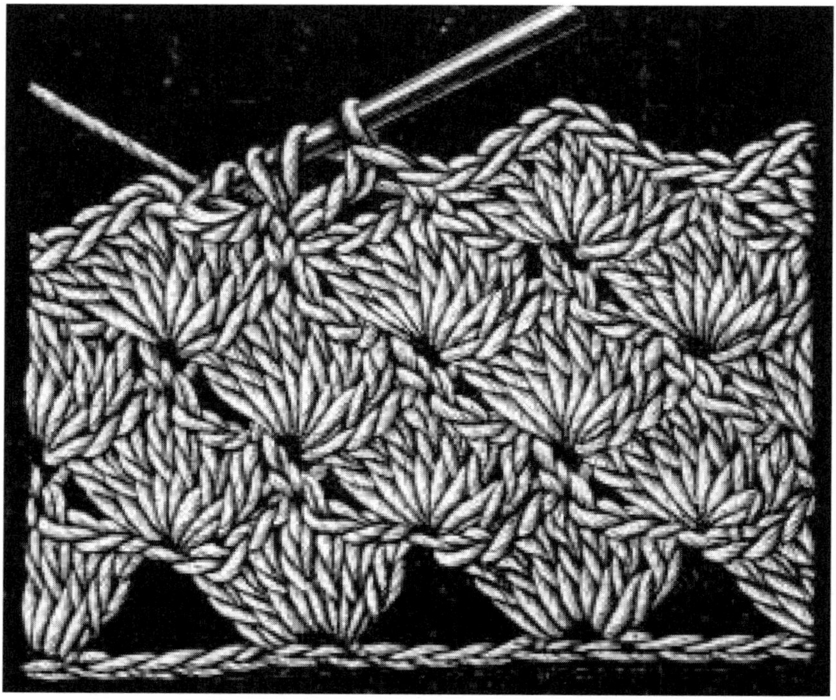

Figure 433

Close shell stitch

(Fig. 433).—This pretty stitch, which can only be worked in rows all one way, is more especially suitable for children's jackets and petticoats. It is easy, and has the merit of being quickly done. On a foundation chain, or other stitches, make 2 chains, 7 double crochets on the 4th stitch, * 1 chain, 7 double crochets on the 5th stitch of the last row, and repeat from *.

2nd row—** 7 double crochets on the chain stitch of the last row which connects 7 bars, then make 1 slip stitch on the 4th of the 7 double crochets of the first row and repeat from **.

Picots

The edges of most crochet work are ornamented with picots, or small points of different shapes, called close picots, chain picots, and lace picots.

Close picots may be subdivided into large and small, pointed and rounded, picots with rounded leaves, and picots with pointed leaves.

Small rounded picots.—These be made either separately and then sewn on, or at once, on to a crochet border. In the first case, begin with 3 chains, then coming back, make 1 slip stitch on the second and on the first chain stitch. In the second case, make 1 chain, take the needle out of the stitch and put it in from the right side, under both edges of the last stitch, take up the dropped stitch, bring it to the right side, * 3 chain; then returning: 1 slip stitch on each chain, draw the needle out, put it in from the right side into the second stitch of the row beneath, take up the loop, bring it back to the right side, and repeat from *.

Large rounded picots.—5 chain, skip 3, 1 double crochet on the 2nd, and 1 double crochet on the 1st chain stitch.

When you want to attach these picots at once to an existing piece of work, drop the last loop and bring it back again with the needle from the wrong side to the right and skip 2 stitches, instead of one, as in the case of the small picots.

Pointed picots.—Cast on 6 chain, then returning, and skipping the 6th stitch: 1 single stitch, 1 slip stitch, 1 half double crochet, 1 treble, and 1 treble.

Picots with rounded leaves.—* 4 chain, and 3 double crochets on the first stitch, and 1 single on the same stitch on which the double crochets were, **, or 6 chain and repeat from * to **.

When these picots serve as a finish to a straight edge, make 2 single stitches in the preceding row instead of 2 chain.

Picots with pointed leaves.—6 chain, on the first chain stitch: 3 trebles, of which you retain the two last loops on the hook, 1 over, draw the thread through the 4 loops, 5 chain, 1 single on the stitch where the double crochets are.

Chain picots.—For the small chain picots, make 5 chain and 1 slip stitch on the first of these 5 stitches. For the large ones, 5 chain and 1 double crochet on the first stitch.

Picots in bullion stitch (see figs. 424 and 425, p. 26).—5 chain, 1 double crochet in bullion stitch drawn up into a ring, and joined to the 5th chain stitch.

Drooping picots (Fig. 434, p. 36).—5 chain, drop the loop, put the needle into the first of the 5 chain stitches, take up the dropped loop, and draw it through the stitch.

Figure 434

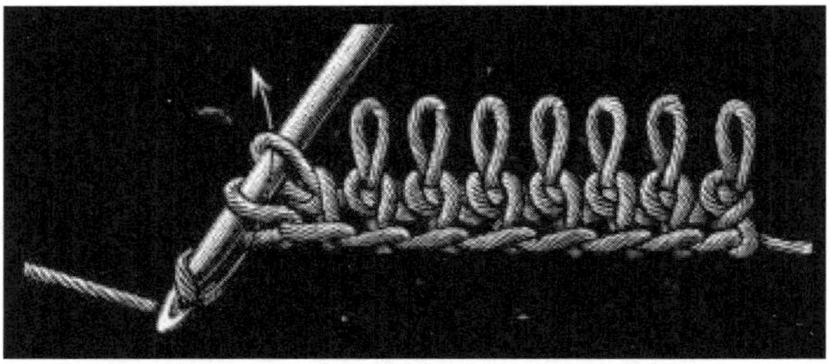

Figure 435

Figure 436

Lace picots (Figs. 435 and 436).—Fig. 435 represents picots formed of chain stitches, as follows: 2 chain, put the needle into the first, 1 over, bring the thread back to the front, 2 chain: * put the needle into the two loops, and at the same time, into the second loop and the first chain, draw the thread through in a loop, then make 2 chain and repeat from *.

In order to make the picots more even and regular, it is advisable to form them over a coarse knitting needle or mesh.

Fig. 436 represents picots attached by slip stitches to the edge of a finished piece of work. This is done as follows: Make 1 slip stitch, draw out the loop to the proper length for a picot, and slip it on a mesh. Then put the needle into the horizontal parts of the last stitches, turn the thread round the needle, draw it through in a loop, and make 1 slip stitch on the next stitch, and so on.

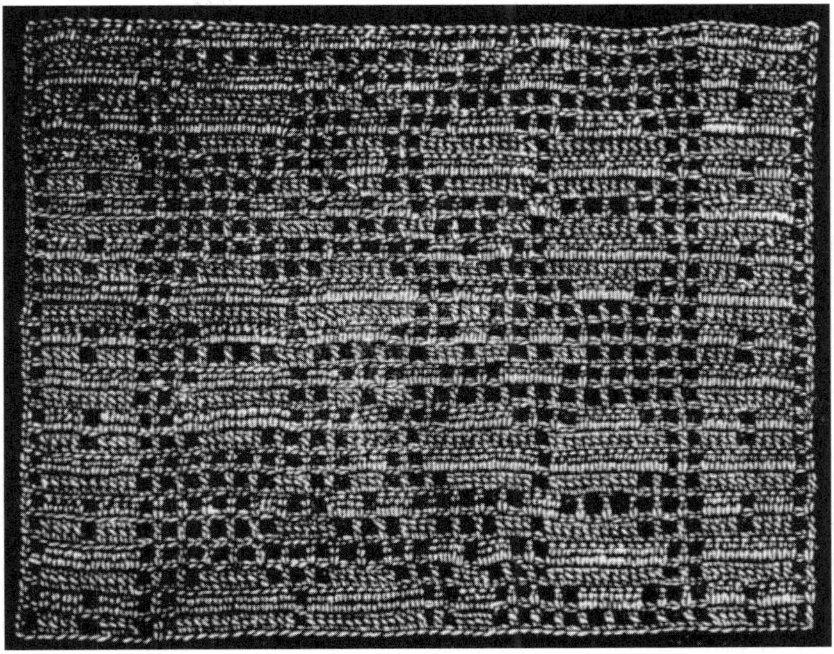

Figure 437

Method for copying tapestry patterns in crochet work

(Figs. 437 and 438).—Printed cross stitch and embroidery patterns can very well be copied in crochet work especially when they are in two colors only, or rather, are drawn in one color, on a slip background.

These patterns are copied in crochet by means of chain stitches and double crochets, which, rising one above the other in rows, form little squares. For each square marked on the pattern, you must count, in the grounding, 1 double crochet and 2 chain stitches; in the solid parts, 3 double crochets.

The squares formed by the chain stitches should always begin and end with a treble.

When, a solid square comes between empty or foundation squares, count 4 double crochets for the solid square, because the last double crochet of the last empty square touches the third double crochet of the solid one.

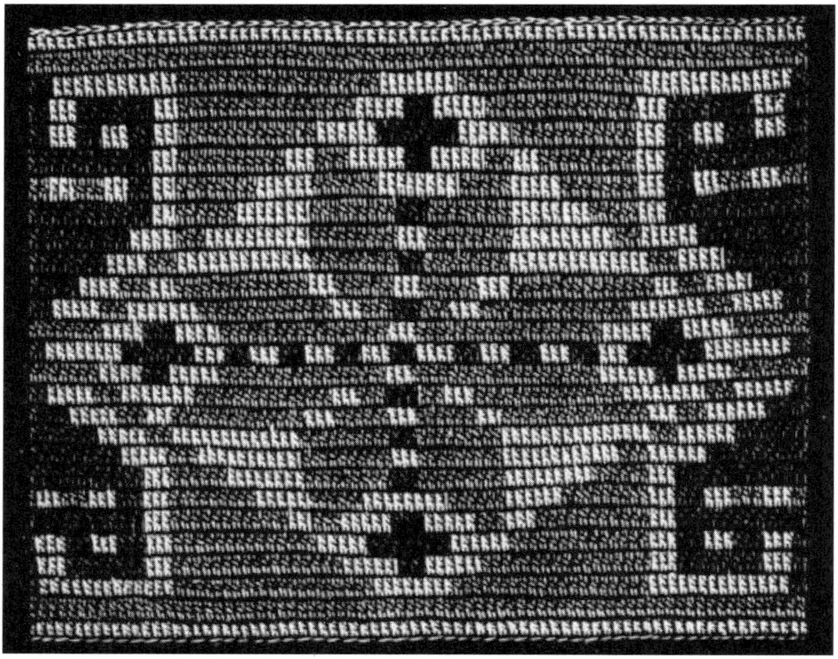

Figure 438

Thus, for 2 solid squares, side-by-side, count 7 double crochets, and for 3 squares, count 10. Embroidery patterns worked in several colors can be reproduced in crochet either by double crochets and rows worked one way only, cutting off the thread at the end of each row, or by slip stitches, worked in rows back and forth.

When only three colors are used, pass two threads under the stitches; when more than three, leave those which are not in use at the back of the work and only bring them to the front as they are wanted. The thread you lay aside takes the place of the thread in use. Of course, the threads not in use can only can be disposed of in this way when the work has a wrong side; otherwise they must be passed underneath the stitches. The colors should alternate in the order the pattern prescribes; moreover, the last stitch before you take another color cannot be finished with the same thread. You must pass the new thread through the last loop and draw it up with that.

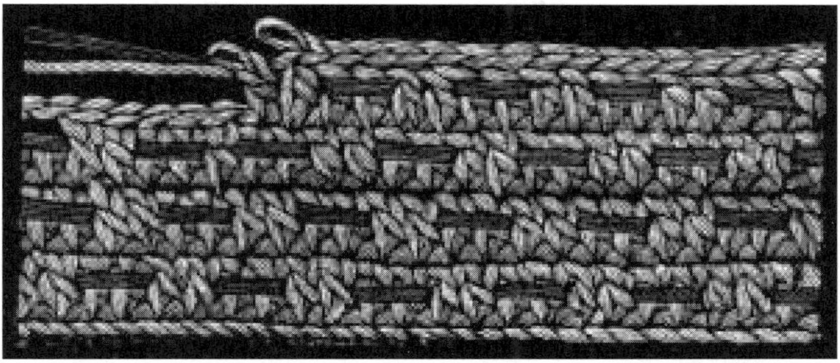

Figure 439

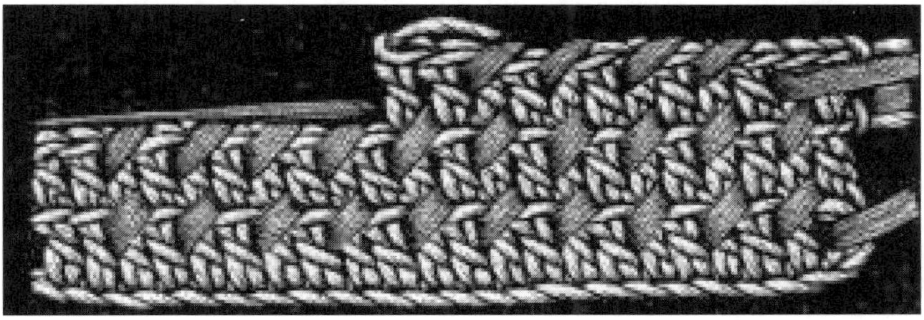

Figure 440

Crochet with Soutache or Lacet (braid)

(Figs. 439 and 440).—These are two patterns of crochet, worked with ordinary crochet cottons and with Soutache or Lacet DMC (a material which has not been used for crochet work before).

Both patterns are worked entirely with double crochets; in fig. 439, the red braid passes over and under 2 double crochets; in fig. 440, it is brought from the wrong side to the right after every 2 double crochets, and passed between them, in such a manner as to form a slanting stitch between the rows of stitches.

Materials: Coton à tricoter DMC Nos. 6 to 12 or Cordonnet 6 fil DMC Nos. 3 to 10. Soutache DMC No. 2 or 3 or Lacets superfins DMC Nos. 2 to 5. **Colors:** The cotton: white or écru. The Soutache or Lacet: Rouge-Cardinal 347, or Rouge-Grenat 326, or Bleu-Indigo 312.[A]

Figure 441

Crochet square

(Fig. 441).—Begin with 4 chain stitches and work 1 single on the 1st chain to make a round. Work 1 chain and 2 slip stitches on the next chain, 3 slip on each of the next 3 chain, then make 1 slip on the stitch on which the two first slip stitches are worked.

Slip the next stitch; that is, put the needle in between the horizontal bars of the 1st slip stitch of the previous row, and draw the thread out without making a stitch.

Then make 1 chain and 2 slip stitches on the slipped stitch.

After that, make 3 slip stitches on the second of the 3 slip that form the corner, and 1 slip on all the other stitches of the last row. The beginning and end of each row, are worked as described above.

Fig. 441 represents a square, worked in consecutive rows. In making a crochet square, the rows may end in the middle of a side.

When you use a stitch that has to be worked back and forth, you turn your work at the end of every row and work back along the stitches you have just made.

Figure 442

Crochet hexagon

(Fig. 442).—Make a foundation chain of 6 stitches and join the round; make 12 slip stitches on the 6 chain; finish the row as indicated for the previous figure == turn the work == * 1 slip, 3 slip on the second slip of the last row; repeat 5 times from *. Finish the row with 1 single stitch == turn the work == 2 slip, 3 slip on the second of the first 3 slip; 3 slip and so on. These hexagons can be made of any size.

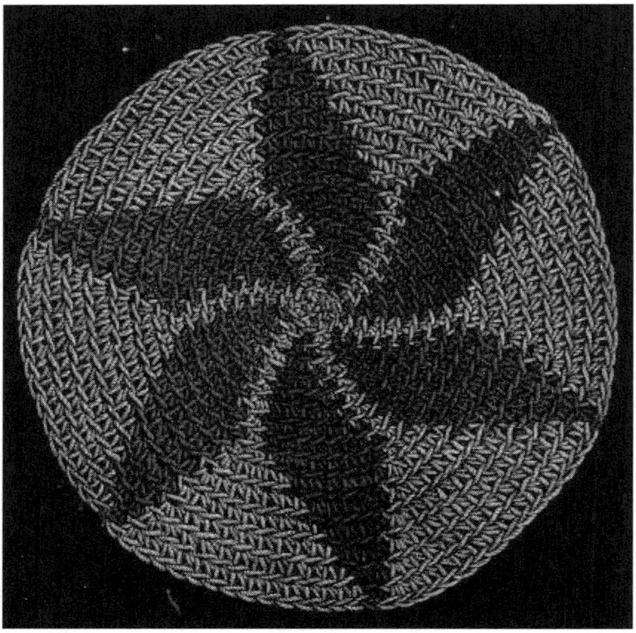

Figure 443

Colored star worked into a light ground

(Fig. 443).—Begin with 3 chain, join the ring = 2 slip on each of the 3 chain; then for the foundation, 1 slip with the dark thread, and 1 with the light on each of the 6 slip.

In each subsequent row, make one more dark stitch, increasing regularly, that is, making 2 stitches on the last light stitch that comes before the dark ones.

Proceed in this manner until you have 6 or 8 dark stitches in all and then begin to decrease in every row by one, until there is only one dark stitch remaining.

These stars are used in the making of purses, cap-crowns, and mats for lamps, etc.

Tunisian crochet

Tunisian crochet is also called crochet-knitting because you have to cast on all the first row of stitches, as in knitting.

Materials: Every kind of cotton, as well as wool and silk, can be used for Tunisian crochet. The stitches look equally well in all these materials, but for things that require frequent washing or cleaning, a easily washable material should be selected, such as Coton à tricoter DMC and Cordonnet 6 fils DMC[A], both strong and suitable in all ways.

As we have already said, Tunisian crochet is done with a long, straight needle with a knob at one end, and it can only be worked on the right side.

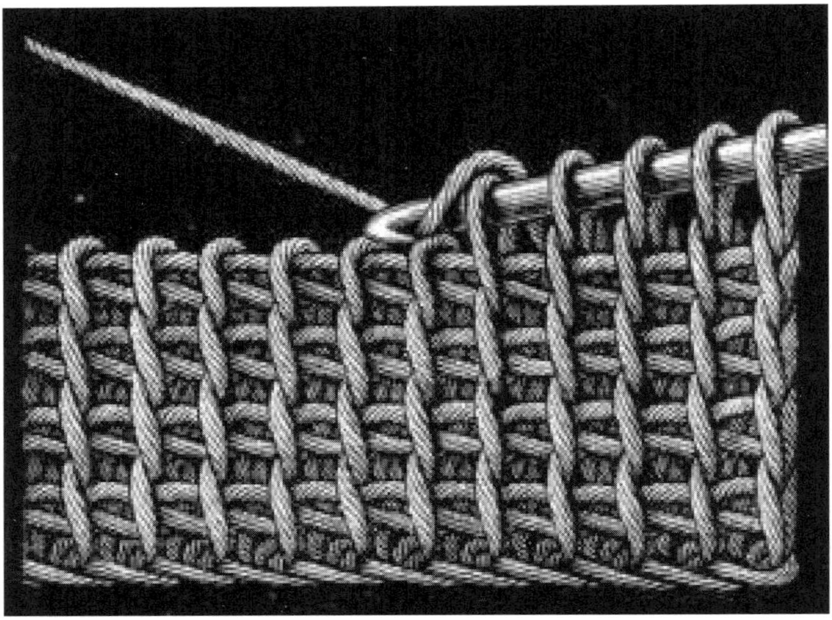

Figure 444

Slip Tunisian crochet

(Fig. 444).—After making a foundation chain of the required length, begin the first, or loop row as it is called. Put the needle into the 2nd chain stitch, draw a loop through and so on, until you have taken up all the chain stitches on the needle. After having made the last stitch of the loop row, make 1 chain stitch and then pass to the second row that completes the stitch. Turn the thread round the needle, draw it through two loops, turn the thread round again, and again draw it through two loops, and so on to the end.

Figure 445

Straight plaited Tunisian stitch

(Fig. 445).—Skip the first loop in the 1st row, take up the second, and come back to the first, so that the 2 loops are crossed. Work the second row in the same manner as the second row of the preceding figure.

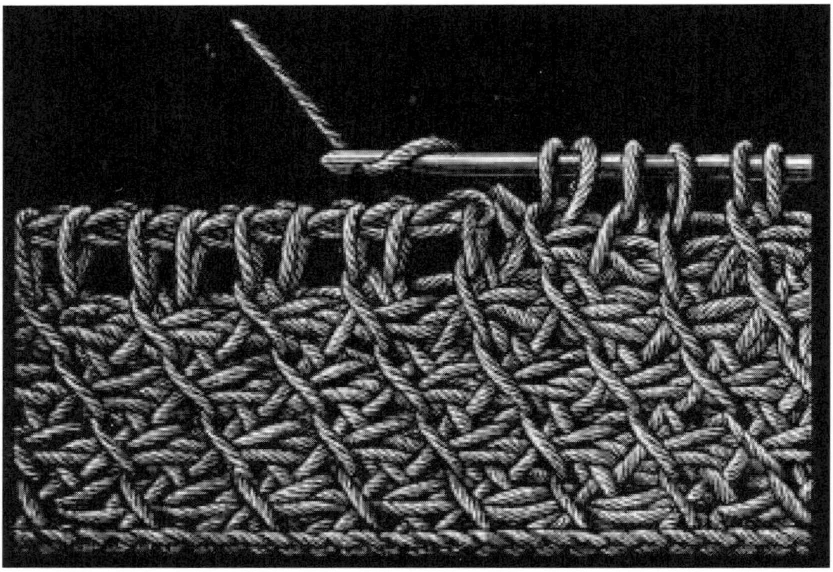

Figure 446

Diagonal plaited Tunisian stitch

(Fig. 446).—This stitch like the preceding one, taking up first the second loop and then the first. The second row is also worked in the same way as the preceding stitch. In the third row, take up the first stitch and draw the third through the second, so as to produce diagonal lines across the surface of the work.

Open Tunisian stitch

This is an easy kind of Tunisian crochet. The first row is worked as in fig. 444. In the row of slip stitches, you alternately join 2 and 3, or 3 and 4 loops of the preceding row together, and replace them with as many chain stitches.

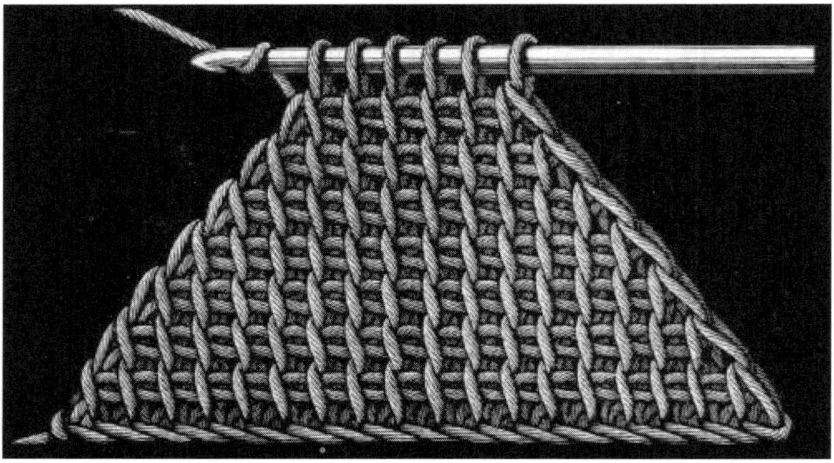

Figure 447

Decreasing and increasing in Tunisian crochet

(Fig. 447). Our illustration shows how to decrease on both sides and by that means to form scallops.

Skip a stitch alternately on the right and left. On the right you crochet the first two stitches together, and at the end of the row, the last two, and so on, to the end. You increase in the same order, first on the right, and then on the left.

Figure 448

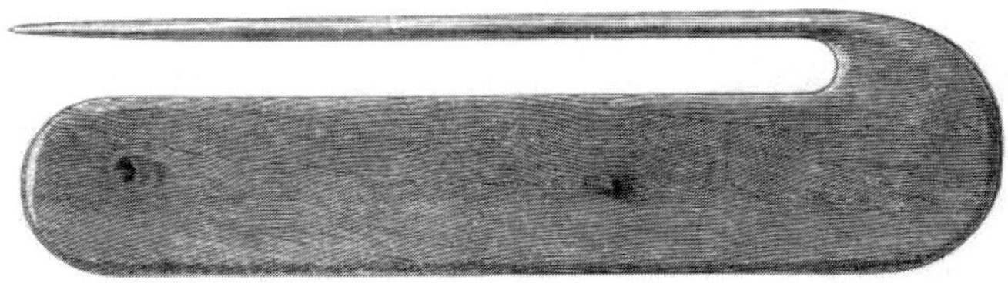

Figure 449

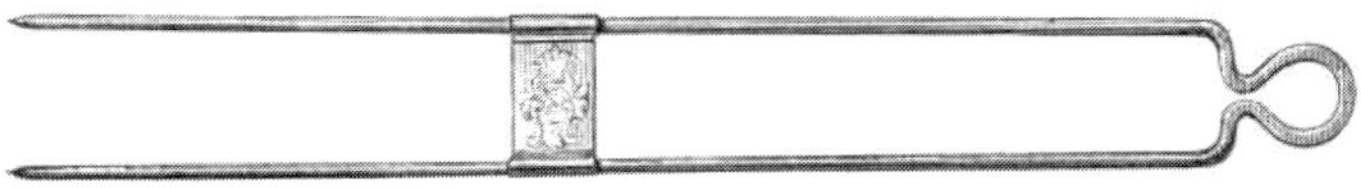

Figure 450

Hairpin crochet

(Figs. 448, 449, 450).—The hairpin crochet is so called because it is worked on a kind of large steel hairpin or fork with two or more prongs. Wooden and nickel varieties of this implement are also used.

Very pretty laces, fringes, gimp headings, and the like can be made in this kind of crochet work. It is often used in combination with ordinary crochet and slip and scalloped braids and gimps, or as a heading for fringes made of tufts and pendant balls. There are many stitches that can be worked in hairpin crochet. We shall only describe those here that will best teach our readers how the work is done.

Materials: For washable laces, Cordonnet 6 fils DMC is the best; for furniture fringes, the lower numbers of Coton à tricoter DMC; and for producing the appearance of filoselle, the lower numbers of Coton à repriser DMC are to be taken.

Stitches: Begin with a chain stitch, made with an ordinary crochet needle. Take the needle out of the loop, and insert the left prong of the fork upward from below, holding the fork between the thumb and finger of the left hand. The thread should always be in front. Then put the thread over the right prong, and put the needle into the loop on the left prong. Take

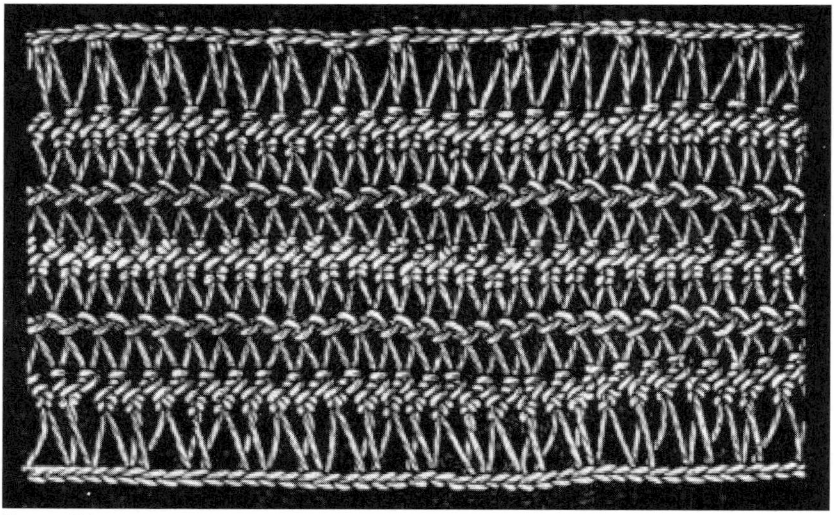

Figure 451

up the thread, draw it through the loop, put the thread over the needle, and draw it through the loop that is on the needle. Twist the loop round the left prong, turn the needle round to the right (the thread will now be wound round the right prong); put the needle into the loop on the left prong, throw the thread over the needle, draw it through, tighten the loops, and so on.

These stitches may be doubled, or you may make several double crochets on each loop, or arrange the slip stitches in different ways.

Hairpin insertion (Fig. 451): Begin by making stripes with the fork, covering each thread with two slip stitches. Then join the stripes together by the loops, drawing the left loop over the right one and the right one over the left. When you come to the end of the stripes fasten off the last loops by a few stitches. To strengthen the edges, join two loops together by 1 slip, 2 chain, 1 slip and so on.

Materials: Fil à pointer DMC No. 20 or 30, or Cordonnet 6 fils DMC Nos. 4 to 15, white or écru.[A]

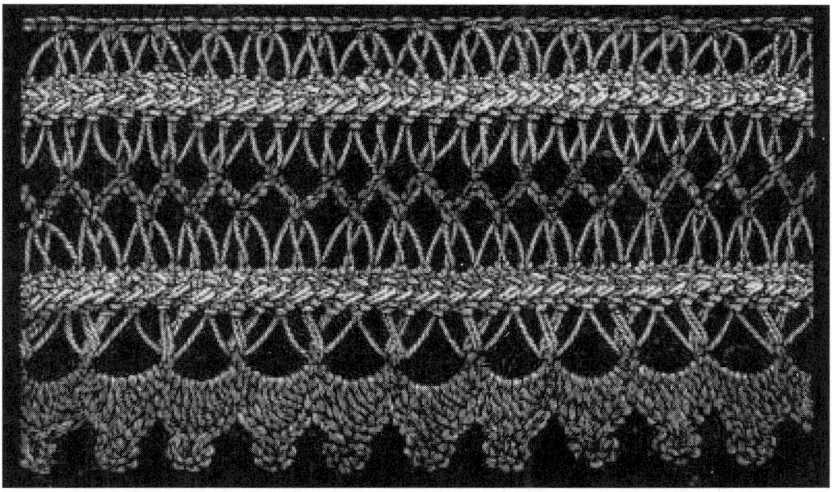

Figure 452

Hairpin lace

(Fig. 452).—When, by making two half double crochets in each loop, you have got the necessary length of hairpin crochet, join the loops two and two with a contrasting colored thread. Work 1 slip stitch joining 2 loops on the right, 2 chain, 1 slip joining the 2 loops on the left; then 2 chain and come back to the right, and so on, until you have taken up all the loops. This forms the zigzag in the middle.

Materials: For the hairpin work: Fil à pointer DMC Nos. 20 to 30, or Cordonnet 6 fils DMC Nos. 3 to 10, white or écru. For the edge. Coton à tricoter DMC Nos. 16 to 30. Colors: Rouge-Cardinal 347, or Jaune-Rouille 364, or Brun-Marron 406.[A]

1st row—join 3 loops by 1 slip, 5 chain.

2nd row—on the 5 chain stitches, make 1 slip, 1 half double crochet, 3 double crochets, 1 picot, made with 5 chain (for the chain picots, see p. 237), 1 half double crochet, 1 slip. The footing of this lace is made like the one in fig. 451.

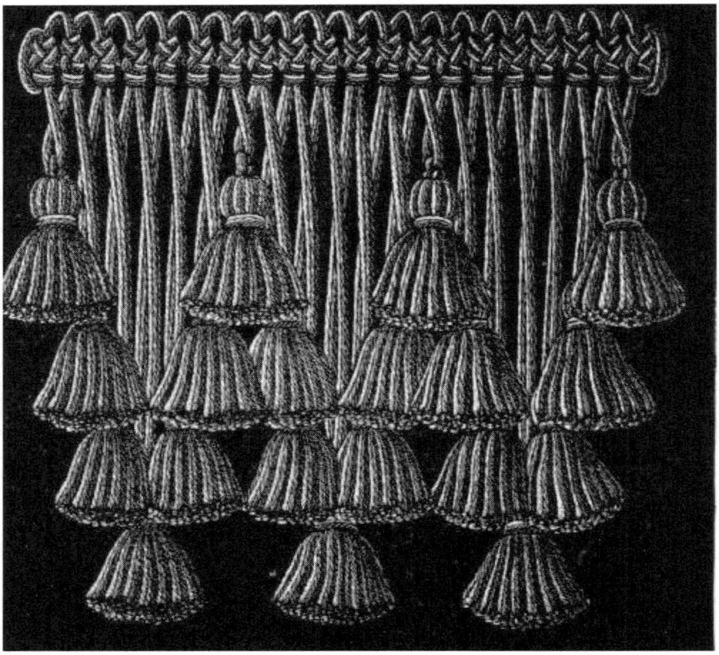

Figure 453

Hairpin fringes

(Figs. 453, 454, 455, 456).—Fig. 453 is made with a fork composed of one branch and 3 or 4 rulers, round which the thread is wound in succession to form loops of different lengths. Use for either a single very coarse thread, or else several fine threads used together as one.

The heading of the fringe is slip, and heavy tassels are fastened into the loops. The tassels are made as follows: take a thick skein of the same thread the fringe is made of, pass it through the loop, leaving just the length required for the tassel at one end. Thread a needle with the same thread and twist it round the skein at the right distance from the top to form the head of the tassel; then cut the ends even at the bottom. Because the loops are of different lengths, the tassels will hang in steps, and the fuller and heavier they are, the handsomer the fringe will be.

Fig. 454 represents another pattern of fringe. The first part is made with the same fork as the preceding one, but instead, however, of winding the thread round the several prongs in succession, pass it alternately round the two first and the fourth, making loops of only two different lengths. The length of the tassels depends on these loops and may be varied in the

Figure 454

second row by adding balls made to the middle, or by long meshes, which are made over the whole width of the fork and affixed to the loops.

Figs. 455 and 456 (next page) represent two pretty patterns of fringes made of écru cotton with a strong twist. These patterns are easily washable.

The loops in fig. 455 are all of one length, and a ball hangs from every third one. Two chapters ago, a minute description was given of the way in which these balls are made. The heading of the loops is formed by a row of chain stitches, varying in number from four to six, according to the size of the cotton. The edge is ornamented with little picots. The fringe shown in fig. 456, consists of three long loops alternating with three short loops, which causes the balls that connected to them to form two parallel lines.

If you join the loops of the heading together, three and three, you will have to make enough chain stitches to cover the space that between them.

The picots are made with 6 chain stitches. Put the needle back into the fifth stitch after closing the picot, make 1 chain, 2 slip, in the preceding row, then 1 picot and so on.

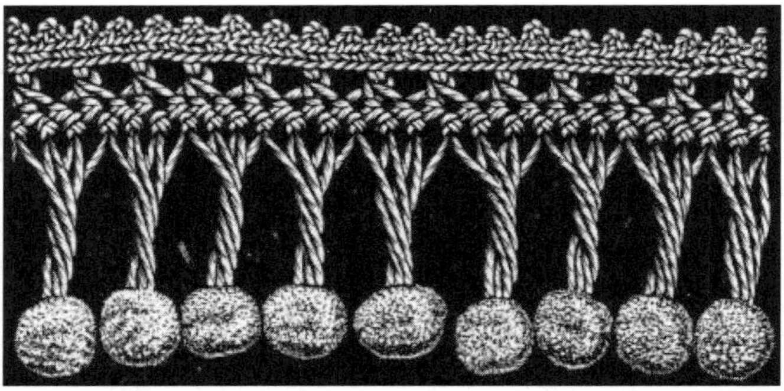

Figure 455

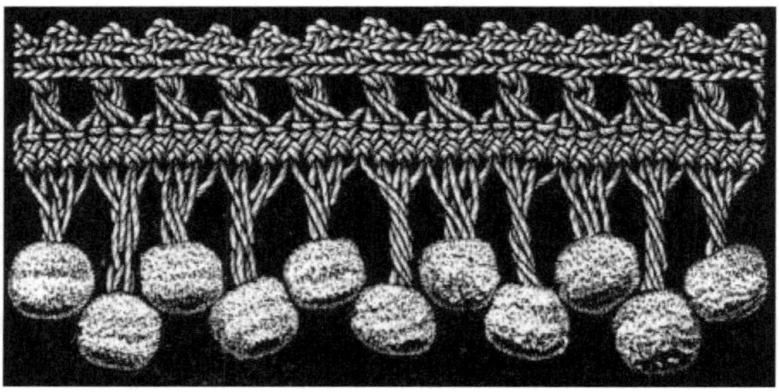

Figure 456

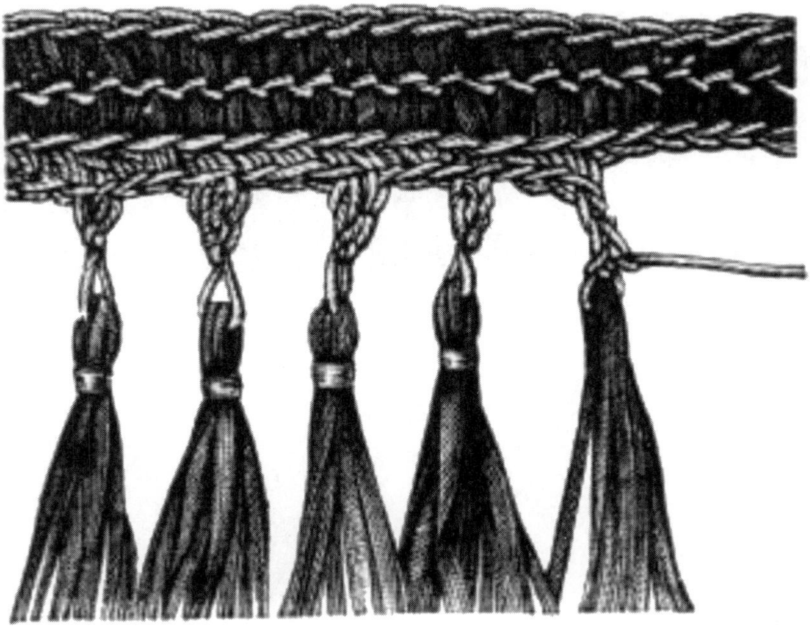

Figure 457

Fringe made with Lacet or braid

(Fig. 457).—This is an easy fringe to make and a very effective trimming for tablecloths and curtains; it is also embroidered on coarse materials.

Begin with a foundation chain in a coarse écru twist. Make the light stitch in the middle of the heading of the fringe from the same material.

In the next row, use the twist and the braid together as follows: Make the twist* 1 chain stitch and put the needle into the first stitch of the foundation chain. Take up the braid, draw it through, turn the twist round the needle, then draw it through the braid and the chain stitch. To make the braid loops longer, they may be made over a wooden ruler. To the two rows of braid stitches, represented in the pattern, you may add as many other rows as you please. On the fringed side, make 4 slip, 3 chain. Draw out one very long loop and fasten into it a cluster of lengths of braid from 10 to 12 cm (4 to 4¾ in.) long, and draw the loop tightly round it to secure the tassel. Make 3 slip on the chain stitches. Repeat from *.

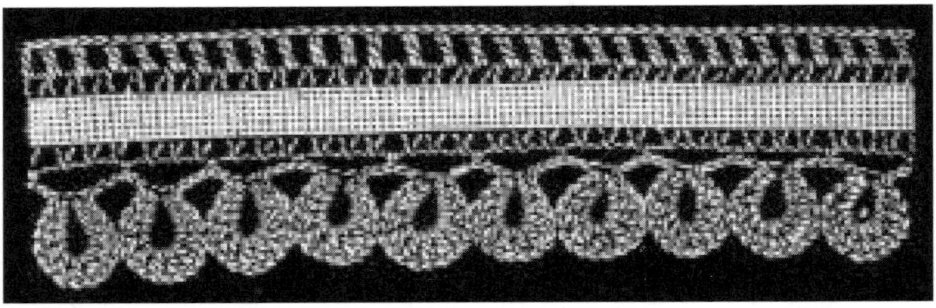

Figure 458

Lace made on Point Lace braid

(Fig. 458).—To make the rounds, stitch 1 slip on the braid, 10 chain; then coming back, make 1 single on the 4th chain.

Materials: Fil d'Alsace DMC Nos. 30 to 50, or Cordonnet 6 fils DMC No. 80, white[A] and Point Lace braid.

In this first round, make 1 chain, 1 half double crochet, 12 double crochets *, 1 half double crochet, 1 chain, 1 single on the 4th chain; 3 chain, and 1 single on the braid, far enough from the 1st chain for the rounds not to overlap each other. Then 10 chain, 1 single on the 4th chain, 1 single, 1 half double crochet, 4 double crochets. Join to the first round between the 8th and 9th double crochets. Make 8 double crochets and repeat from *. For the footing: 1 treble, 1 chain, skip a few threads of the edge of the braid, 1 treble.

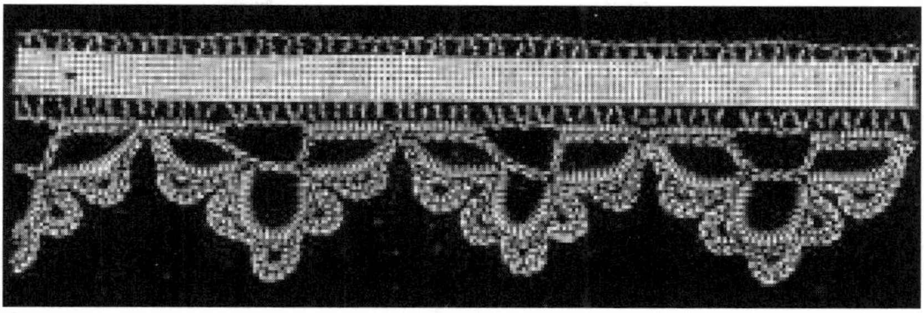

Figure 459

Crochet guipure lace

(Fig. 459).—This charming little lace makes a very good substitute for guipure. It can be made on a row of double crochets just as well as on point lace braid, or on a mignardise after you have raised its picots by single and chain stitches.

Materials: Fil d'Alsace DMC Nos. 70 to 90. Cordonnet 6 fils DMC Nos. 80 to 120, or Fil à dentelle DMC Nos. 40 to 70.

Make 6 slip *, 9 chain, and leave an interval equalling in length 6 bars of the point lace braid used in our pattern. For the braid: 6 slip stitches, very close together, 8 chain, 1 single on the 7th of the 9 chain, 10 chain, 1 single on the 3d of the 9 chain, 8 chain, and 1 slip close to the first of the first 6 slip.

1st scallop—7 slip, 5 chain, join to the 4th chain. On the 5th chain, make 6 slip, and on the 8th chain, make 3 slip.

2nd scallop—on the 10 chain, make 7 slip, 5 chain, join to the 4th chain = on the 5 chain: 6 slip = on the 10 chain, 5 slip, 5 chain, join to the 4th chain, 6 slip, 5 chain, join to the 4th chain, 6 chain, and 1 slip on the 10th chain.

3rd scallop—begin like the first scallop, then repeat from *.

Figure 460

Lace made on Point Lace braid

(Fig. 460).—On the braid, work a row of double crochets 1 or 2 chain stitches apart, according to the size of the braid, and on this row of double crochets, make two other rows as follows:

1st row—5 chain, 1 double crochet on the double crochet of the preceding row, 5 chain, 1 double crochet on the same stitch to which the first double crochet is joined, 5 chain, skip 3 double crochets, 1 double crochet on the 4th double crochet of the row beneath.

2nd row—1 slip on the 3rd of the 5 first chain, 3 slip, 1 double crochet on the 3rd of the chain stitches between the two double crochets of the first row that come close together; 3 chain, 1 double crochet on the same stitch, 3 chain, 1 double crochet on the same stitch, 3 chain, 1 double crochet on the 3rd of the next 5 chain.

Materials: The same as for Fig. 458.

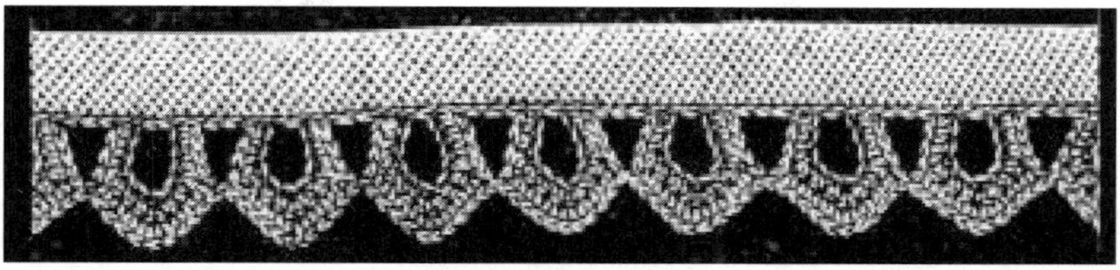

Figure 461

Crochet lace

(Fig. 461).—**1st row**—3 slip close together, in the braid; * 13 chain, join to the 1st slip. On each of the first 6 chain; 1 slip; = on the 7th chain: 3 slip, then on the other chain stitches: 6 slip. In the braid: 7 slip and repeat from *.

2nd row—* skip 2 slip on the first row, 5 slip to reach the 2nd stitch added in the first row, 4 slip on the 2nd added stitch, 4 slip on the next stitches. Repeat from *.

Materials: Lacet superfin DMC No. 14 and Fil d'Alsace DMC Nos. 30 to 70.[A]

To make an insertion, drop the thread after the 2nd of the 4 stitches at the point and then put the needle into the stitch of the finished stripe, take up the thread again, and draw it through the stitch. Proceed to the second side of the scallop.

Figure 462

Crochet lace with mignardise

(Fig. 462).—This and all the patterns that follow, up to fig. 473, make very useful trimmings. Begin by raising the picots on both sides of the mignardise with 1 slip stitch and 1 chain.

Materials: Depending on the mignardise used, either Fil d'Alsace DMC Nos. 30 to 70, or Fil à dentelle DMC Nos. 25 to 70.[A]

To make the rows of crochet work between the lace, make 1 double crochet on 1 chain, 4 chain, skip 2 picots of the mignardise, 1 double crochet between the 3rd and 4th picot.

Work the edge in two rows.

1st row—1 double crochet between 2 picots, 3 chain, skip 2 picots, 1 treble.

2nd row—1 double crochet on 3 chain, 3 chain, 1 treble, 3 chain, 3 double crochets, 7 chain, turn back and join to the 1st of the 3 double crochets, 2 chain, join them to the 2nd treble, 2 double crochets on the 7 chain; keep the last loops of the last double crochet on the needle and join them to those of the next treble.

Figure 463

Lace with two rows of leaves

(Fig. 463).—This is one of the most pleasant crochet patterns to work. The leaves are made separately and fastened into a foundation with thread at least two numbers finer than the thread the leaves are made of.

Materials: Fil d'Alsace DMC Nos. 20 to 100, Cordonnet 6 fils DMC Nos. 25 to 80 or Fil à dentelle DMC Nos. 25 to 100.

Leaf with 5 petals: 8 chain, make a ring = 2 slip on the ring = 1st petal * 11 chain, skip 3 chain, 1 half double crochet on the 8th chain, 1 chain, skip the 7th chain, 1 double crochet on the 6th chain, 1 chain, 1 double crochet on the 4th chain, 1 chain, 1 double crochet on the 3rd chain, 2 chain, 2 slip on the ring.

2nd petal: 15 chain, skip 3 chain, 1 half double crochet *, 1 chain, skip 1 chain, 1 double crochet *. Repeat 4 times from * to *; add 1 chain, 2 double crochets on the ring.

3rd petal: 21 chain, skip 3 chain, 1 half double crochet *, 1 chain, skip 1, 1 double crochet *. Repeat 7 times from * to *; add: 1 chain, skip 1, 2 double crochets in the ring.

The 4th petal is to be worked like the 3rd; the 5th like the 1st.

When the 5 petals are finished, make 2 slip stitches on the ring; then on the chain stitches of the 1st petal: 2 slip, 7 double crochets, 2 double crochets on the 10th stitch; then descending again: 7 double crochets, 2 slip, and 3 single on the 3 slip stitches of the ring.

On the 2nd petal work: 3 slip, 10 double crochets, 2 double crochets on the 14th chain, 10 double crochets, 3 slip, 2 single on the 2 double crochets on the ring.

3rd petal: 2 single, 3 slip, 14 double crochets, 2 double crochets on the 20th chain, 14 double crochets, 3 slip, 1 single.

The 4th petal is worked like the 2nd; the 5th like the 1st bur followed by 1 single on the 1st of the 3 chain stitches of the ring.

For the stalk: 14 chain; skip 1, 9 slip on the 9 chain; 6 chain, skip 1, 5 slip on the 5 chain, 4 slip on the chain stitches that are still disengaged, 2 single on the ring, and then fasten the thread off with a few stitches.

When you have enough leaves, join them together by a row of picots, working from left to right as follows: * take the second petal on the right side of a leaf, put the thread into the 12th stitch; make 2 slip, 1 picot, 1 slip on the stitch on which the picot was made = in all the leaves, the 3rd slip before the picot and the 1st after. Meet in the same stitch beneath = 2 slip, 1 picot, 3 slip, 2 chain = on the 8th stitch of the 3rd petal; 1 slip, 2 slip more on the next stitches **, 1 picot, 3 slip. Repeat 6 times from ** and finish with 2 chain.

On the 7th stitch of the 4th petal: 1 slip, 2 slip on the next stitches ***, 1 picot, 3 slip. Repeat 4 times from ***.

On the 5th stitch of the 5th petal: 1 slip, and on the 4 next, 4 slip ****. Repeat from * to ** round each leaf, then instead of a picot, make 4 chain, join between the 1st and 2nd picot, 4 chain, close the picot. From this point the preceding series of stitches takes the place of the picot that immediately follows the sign **; proceed to ****.

Foundation for the footing of the lace, with a single row of leaves.— When all the leaves are joined together, take the finer number of cotton and fasten your thread to the last stitch of the small stalk; then make: * 2 chain, 1 slip on the 9th stitch of the 5th petal; 6 chain, skip 2, 1 slip on the 3rd stitch; 6 chain, 1 slip on the 3rd stitch, 1 chain, 1 slip on the 5th stitch of the 4th petal; 6 chain, 1 slip on the 3rd chain; 2 chain, 1 slip on the 4th stitch (counting from the bottom) of the 5th petal of the next leaf; 3 chain, 1 single on the last stitch of the long stalk; 3 chain, join to the 3rd chain stitch, 3 chain, draw the thread again in coming back, through the 3rd of the second set of 6 chain stitches in the 1st petal; 1 single. Turning back and from left to right: 1 single on the slip stitch between the chain stitches, 6 chain, 1 slip on the 2nd of the last 3 chain; 6 chain, 1 slip on the stalk, 6 chain, 1 slip on the 3rd stitch of the stalk; 6 chain, 1 slip on the 4th stitch of the stalk; 7 chain, 1 slip at the top of the little stalk, and then repeat from *. The network in the next rows, which may be of any width, is composed of 6 chain stitches and 1 slip on the loop of the last row.

For the second to last row of the network, make 4 chain, 1 slip over each loop, and complete the lace by a row of slip stitches.

To make the leaves stand out from the foundation, use two shades of thread: white and écru, white and Jaune-Rouille 365, or white and Gris-Cendre 415.

The following is the way to join two rows of leaves that have previously been edged with picots.

Fasten the thread onto the little stalk, * 3 chain, 1 slip on the 8th stitch of the leaf, 2 chain, join to the middle picot of the 3rd petal of the top leaf; 2 chain, 3 slip on the 5th petal of the bottom row, 1 picot, 3 slip.

For the 2nd petal of the bottom leaf: 3 slip, 1 picot, 3 slip.

For the 5th petal of the next leaf below: 3 slip, 4 chain, 1 single on the long stalk, 5 chain, 1 slip on the 2nd picot of the 1st petal of the preceding leaf, 5 chain, 1 single on the 2nd picot of the 4th petal of the top leaf, 4 chain, 1 slip on the 4th single of the stalk, 3 chain, 1 single on the 7th picot of the 3rd petal of the top leaf, 3 chain, skip 1 stitch of the stalk, 1 slip on the stalk, 3 chain, 1 slip on the 6th picot of the top leaf, 3 chain, 1 slip on the little stalk. Repeat from *.

Three and even four rows of leaves may be joined together in this manner to make a very pretty lace, particularly suitable for linen.

Figure 464

Insertion with waved braid

(Fig. 464).—1 slip stitch at the point of the braid, 7 chain, 1 single on the 2nd chain. On the next chain stitches: 1 half double crochet, 1 treble, 1 treble, 1 double treble, 1 slip on the next point of the braid.

Repeat the same stitches on the second side, except that after the 6th chain stitch, draw the thread through the 7th of the 1st finished row.

Little wheels, set between the crochet pyramids and described in the chapters on filet-guipure and Irish lace, complete the insertion.

Materials: According to the size of the braid, either Fil d'Alsace DMC Nos. 20 to 70, or Cordonnet 6 fils DMC Nos. 40 to 70.[A]

Figure 465

Crochet lace made with leaf braid

(Fig. 465).—Introduce the thread into one of the leaves of the braid and, working from right to left, make for the outer border: * 1 slip, 2 chain, 1 picot in bullion stitch with 5 twists of the thread, 2 chain, 1 double crochet near the end of the leaf. Leave the last 2 loops of the double crochet on the needle **.

Take 2 leaves of the braid and fold them one upon the other. Make 1 double crochet near the stalk of these folded leaves, tighten the loops of the 2 double crochets; chain ***, 1 picot, 2 chain, 1 slip, 2 chain. Repeat 5 times from ***.

Proceed with 1 picot, 2 chain—there will be 7 picots round the folded leaves—1 double crochet on the folded leaves, and repeat from ** to *, then do the inverse, and begin again from *.

Materials: Fil d'Alsace DMC Nos. 50 to 100 or Fil à dentelle DMC Nos. 50 to 80.[A]

For the footing of the lace, 4 rows are required.

1st row—* 1 treble close to the stalk of the leaf, 5 chain, 1 double crochet at the third of the leaf, 1 treble at the 2nd third of the leaf, 5 chain, 2 trebles (one on the right leaf, one on the left). Draw the last loops of the 2 double crochets up together and repeat from *.

2nd row—On each of the little loops formed by the 5 chain of the last row, make 1 slip, 3 chain, 1 picot in bullion stitch, 7 chain, 1 picot, 3 chain; 1 slip on the next loop and so on.

3rd row—1 slip on the 4th of the 7 chain, 5 chain, 1 slip and so on.

4th row—1 slip on each loop of the last row.

Figure 466

Crochet lace made with leaf braid

(Fig. 466).—Begin with the outside edge:

1st row—At the end of a leaf: 1 treble, 6 chain, 1 picot in bullion stitch, 6 chain, 1 double crochet = at the beginning of a 2nd leaf: 6 chain, 1 picot, 6 chain, 1 double crochet at the end of the leaf = 7 chain, 1 picot, 7 chain, 1 double crochet on the 3rd leaf = 6 chain, 1 picot, 6 chain, 1 double crochet at the end of the 3rd leaf = 6 chain, 1 treble, 6 chain, 1 double crochet on the 4th leaf = 1 treble joined to the 4th and 1st leaf of the next scallop = 1 double crochet at the end of the 1st leaf, join and draw the last loops of these 3 double crochets together.

2nd row—over each double crochet and picot: * 1 slip, 3 chain, 1 picot, 7 chain, 1 picot, 3 chain, 1 slip = repeat 6 times from *.

At the indent and before the last picot: 2 chain, 1 picot, 2 chain = 1 slip before the 1st picot of the next scallop.

3rd row—1 treble, 8 chain, repeat 6 times. In the indent join the 4th of the 7 chain stitches right and left together by 1 treble.

4th row—15 single on each loop of 8 chain.

Materials: Cordonnet 6 fils DMC Nos. 40 to 80 or Fil à dentelle Nos. 50 to 80.[A]

Inside junction.—Begin at the edge of the first leaf, fasten on the thread and make 10 chain and 1 treble at the end of the leaf; then 1 double treble, and draw up both together, 5 chain, 2 double trebles on the leaves to the right and left = 5 chain, 2 double trebles, one at the end and the other at the beginning of the 3rd and 4th leaf = 2 chain, 1 picot in bullion stitch, 2 chain, 1 slip on the last stitch of the first double crochets, 10 chain, 1 slip on the last stitch of the last double crochets; 5 chain, 1 double treble at the end of the 4th leaf.

Going back to the beginning: 5 chain, 1 single on the 10 chain above the picot = 5 chain, 1 single on the 5th of the first 10 chain = 12 chain, 1 slip on the loop of the last double treble, 7 chain, 1 picot in bullion stitch, 6 chain = 1 slip on the stalk between the 2 leaves; 6 chain, 1 picot, 7 chain, 1 double treble on the leaf, 5 chain, repeat from *.

2nd row—5 chain, 1 double crochet on the lower loops. Distribute the chain stitches equally.

3rd row—1 slip in the braid that forms the footing of the lace, 2 chain, 1 slip on the last chain stitches, 2 chain, 1 slip in the braid, continuing in this pattern to join the crochet work and the braid together.

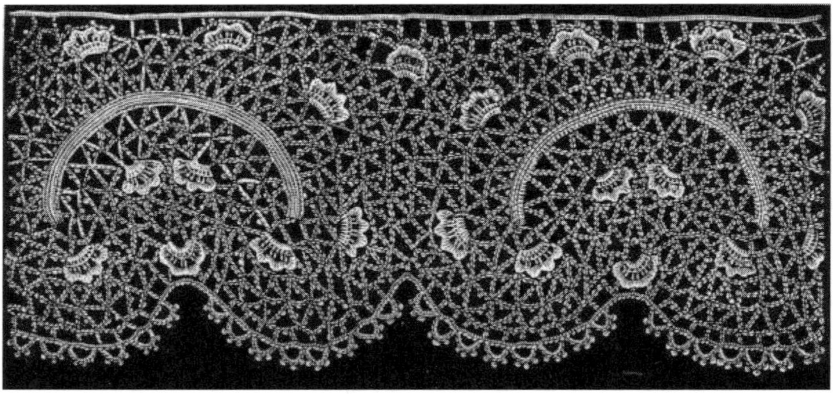

Figure 467

Irish lace

(Fig. 467).—Begin with the semicircles in the middle of the pattern, which arch over two scallops, and cast on 117 chain. Then lay a double or threefold thread of Cordonnet 6 fils DMC No. 2 over the chain stitches and make one slip stitch on each; then cut the padding thread short off.

Materials: Cordonnet 6 fils DMC Nos. 25 to 100, Fil à pointer DMC No. 30 or Fil d'Alsace DMC Nos. 30 to 100.[A]

On the other side of the chain, make 2 slip, * 2 chain, 1 picot, 7 chain, 1 picot, 2 chain, skip 7; 1 slip on each of the 2 next stitches **.

Repeat 11 times from * to **; the 11th time making only 6 chain.

2nd and 3rd row—On the upper side, over a double thread of twist: 1 slip on each stitch of the last row; cut off the padding thread = 2 chain, 1 picot, 7 chain, 1 picot, 2 chain, 1 slip on the 4th of the 7 chain stitches after the first picot of the preceding row = 3 chain, 1 picot, 3 chain, 1 slip on the 4th of the next 7 chain stitches **. Repeat 11 times from * to ** and then make: 2 chain, 1 picot, 7 chain, 1 picot, 2 chain, 1 slip.

On the upper side and without a padding thread: 3 slip, 1 picot, * 5 slip, 1 picot, **. Repeat 20 times from * to **. Continue with 3 slip, 10 chain, 1 picot, 2 chain, 2 slip on the 4th of the first 7 chains of the 2nd row on the inside of the semicircle = 2 chain, 1 picot, 7 chain, 1 picot, 2 chain, 1 slip on the slip stitch of the previous row = 1 slip on the 1st of the 3 chain = 2 chain, 1 picot, 7 chain, 1 picot, 2 chain, 2 slip as before, = 2 chain, 1 picot, 7 chain, 1 picot, 2 slip = 2 chain, 1 picot, 9 chain, 1 slip. Return and make on the 9 chain: 7 slip, 2 chain, 1 picot, 2 chain, 2 slip = make 4 more scallops like the previous one = 2 chain, 1 picot, 9 chain, 1 slip = return and make on the 9 chain: 7 slip, 2 chain, 1 picot, 2 chain, 2 slip = make 2 more scallops and then a 3rd joined to the scallop that terminates the semicircle on the right by the 2 slip stitches = 2 chain, 1 picot, 7 chain, 1 picot, 2 chain, 2 slip on the point of the crescent = 22 scallops consisting of: 2 chain, 1 picot, 7 chain, 1 picot, 2 chain, 2 slip.

9 slip on the scallop that terminates the semicircle on the left, 7 chain, 2 slip on the next scallop, 2 chain, 1 picot, 2 chain, 2 slip on the next scallop = make 2 bars more of the same kind = 7 chain, 2 slip = 3 bars like the previous ones = 7 chain, 2 slip = 3 bars as before = 2 slip, 7 chain, 7 slip on the next scallop = 1 bar consisting of 3 chain, 1 picot, 3 chain, 2 slip over all the scallops of the preceding row (24 scallops in all).

4th row—3 chain *, 8 double crochets on the 7 chain that follow the 7 slip = turn the work = 1 single on the last treble, 3 chain, 1 double crochet on the 7th and 1 on the 6th of the 8 double crochets, 2 chain, 1 double crochet on the 5th and 1 on the 4th of the 8 double crochets, 2 chain, 1 double crochet on the 3rd and 1 on the 2nd of the 8 double crochets, 3 chain, 1 single on the 1st of the 8 double crochets = turn the work = ** on the 3 chain: 1 slip, 1 half double crochet, 1 treble, 1 half double crochet, 1 slip = 1 slip between the 2 double crochets below = on the 2 chain, 1 slip, 1 half double crochet, 1 treble, 1 half double crochet, 1 slip *** = 1 slip between the 2 double crochets beneath, repeat from *** to **, therefore the reverse way.

Go on with 2 scallops consisting of 2 chain, 1 picot, 7 chain, 1 picot, 2 chain, 2 slip = after the 2nd scallop: 2 chain, 1 picot, 5 chain = 8 double crochets on the 7 chain over the 7 slip, and finish the little flowers consisting of 4 scallops each like the first from * to *** and from *** to ** = 2 slip to get back to the scallop = 1 chain, 1 picot, 2 chain, 2 slip, 3 chain, 1 picot, 7 chain, 1 picot, 2 chain, 2 slip, 3 chain, 1 picot, 3 chain, and make a 3rd flower of 4 scallops like the 2 others = 2 single to come back to the scallop, 2 chain, 1 picot, 2 chain, 2 slip = 2 more scallops like the previous ones, then make the 4th flower of 4 scallops, which must come before the 7 slip stitches of the previous row = 20 scallops consisting of: 2 chain, 1 picot, 7 chain, 1 picot, 2 chain, 2 slip = the last scallop is to be joined to the 1st scallop of the 1st flower, under the left point of the semicircle = 3 single along the small scallop, 3 double crochets, 2 chain, 1 picot, 2 chain, 2 slip on the point of the scallop = 3 bars like the previous ones to be joined to the 2 next scallops = 3 similar bars between the small scallops = 1 single on the scallop between the 2 flowers and 1 single on the 2nd set of chain stitches in the scallop that precedes the 3rd flower = 1 single on the point of the 1st scallop of the 3rd flower = continue the little bars along the 2nd side until past the 4th flower = after the 4th flower make 2 bars consisting of 2 chain, 1 picot, 2 chain, 2 slip = 3 chain, 1 picot, 3 chain, 2 slip on the next scallop **** 7 chain, 2 slip on the next scallop, 3 chain, 1 picot, 3 chain, 2 slip on the next scallop, 3 chain, 1 picot, 3 chain, 2 slip on the next scallop, 3 chain, 1 picot, 3 chain, 2 slip on the next scallop ***** repeat five times from **** to *****. At the 2nd repetition, make 1 bar with 1 picot more, so that you have 4 bars instead of 3. At the 5th repetition, decrease by 1 bar so that you have 2 instead of 3.

1 slip on the point of the scallop of the flower, 3 chain, 1 picot, 7 chain, 1 picot, 3 chain, 3 slip, one of which is made on the 2nd slip of the previous row, and the 2nd on the bar of chain stitches = 3 slip, 1 picot, 7 chain, 1 picot, 3 chain, 2 slip = 2 more similar scallops = then 3 chain, 1 picot, 9 chain, 1 slip on the 2nd slip of the previous row = join and on the 9th chain make 7 slip = 3 chain, 1 picot, 3 chain, 2 slip.

Over the 1st little flower inside the semicircles, make 1 scallop like the previous ones = then 3 chain, 1 picot, 7 chain, 2 slip on the 3rd point of the first flower = 2 chain, 2 slip on the 2nd point of the second flower = 6 slip on the scallop and joined to the 3rd point of the first flower = 3 chain, 1 picot, 3 chain = 2 slip = 1 scallop like the previous ones, 2 slip on the 4th point of the small flower, 3 chain, 1 picot, 9 chain, 1 slip = 7 slip over the 9 chain = 3 chain, 1 picot, 3 chain, 2 slip.

Make 7 scallops of: 3 chain, 1 picot, 7 chain, 1 picot, 3 chain, 2 slip, after the 7th scallop make 1 chain only, which must come just before the 7th chain to the left without a picot and above the point of the semicircle.

Over the 7 chain make a flower like the first with 4 scallops = then 3 scallops, 3 chain, 1 picot, 7 chain, 1 picot, 3 chain, 2 slip. Make one more flower with 4 scallops, 3 scallops like the previous ones = a third flower with 4 scallops, 2 chain, 2 slip, one of them above the point of the row beneath, 12 chain, 1 slip over the next scallop = turn the work. Coming back over the row just made, make: 7 slip on the first 7 of the 12 chain, 1 slip on the point of the scallop, 4 chain, 1 picot, 4 chain, 1 slip on the next scallop, carry on the bars over the flowers and scallops, making 1 slip on the scallops of the flower and 2 slip on the other scallops, up to the 5 slip stitches between the 2 flowers underneath the semicircle.

After the slip stitch that joins the last bar, turn the work and make 23 scallops consisting of: 4 chain, 1 picot, 7 chain, 1 picot, 4 chain, 2 slip.

Cut off the thread and fasten it above the semicircle at the slip stitch which precedes the 7 chain without picot. Make the second side like the first = having reached the middle, close to the 5 slip, turn the work = make the half round of bars and fasten off at the 4th scallop of the flower above the semicircle.

Fasten on at the point under the flowers where the work was turned and on the wrong side. From right to left, work 21 scallops consisting of 4 chain, 1 picot, 7 chain, 1 picot, 4 chain, 2 slip = then add: 4 chain, 1 picot, 10 chain, 1 slip above the point of the scallop of the small flower = turn the work: 7 slip over the 10 chain.

22 bars of 3 chain, 1 picot, 3 chain, 2 slip = after the 22nd bar, 10 chain = come back and join to the picot of the 21st bar = 2 chain, 8 double crochets over the 10 chain and complete the flower as before. After the 4th scallop of the flower: 2 chain, 1 single quite close to the 8 double crochets, 3 chain, 2 slip on the next bar, 3 chain, 1 picot, join to the 2nd stitch of the 4th scallop of the flower, 3 chain, carry on the bars the same distance as on the first side.

Footing of the lace—On the chain stitches that follow the 3rd slip stitch, and above the last little figure, make 1 double treble, 6 chain, join to the middle slip stitch = skip 1 scallop, 1 treble, 6 chain = skip 1 scallop, 1 treble, 6 chain, = skip 1 scallop, 1 double treble, 6 chain, = skip 1 scallop of the figure on the left, 1 treble, 6 chain = skip 1 scallop, 1 treble, 6 chain = skip 1 scallop, 1 treble, 6 chain = skip 1 scallop, 1 treble, 6 chain = skip 1 scallop, 1 treble, 6 chain = skip 1 scallop, 1 treble, 6 chain, 1 double treble, 6 chain, 1 triple treble on the next slip stitch. Repeat the whole, reversed, and finish off the footing with a row of slip stitches.

Edge of the lace—Fasten on, where the semicircles join, 1 treble on the first 3 chain stitches of the empty scallop, 5 chain, 1 treble on the next disengaged chain stitches of the half scallop; continue the same on all the chain scallops and distribute the double crochets so that there may be, in all, 13 times 5 chain stitches.

Add 2 double trebles, the last loops of them connected by a slip stitch; the 1st double treble on the 3 last chain stitches of the last scallop, the 2nd on the slip stitch that follows the 1st scallop of the middle figure = 4 chain, 1 double crochet on the slip stitch of the 2nd point. Repeat the same, reversed.

2nd row—On the first 5 chain of the last row: 5 slip = on the next 5 chain: 5 slip = on the 3 chain, leave a space: 5 slip, 12 chain, come back and join to the 8th chain stitch by a single stitch = on the scallop: 4 slip, 1 picot, 3 slip, 1 picot, 4 slip = and so on, until you have 8 points altogether.

The slip stitches must be distributed as follows:

For the 2nd point, in the 4th space 4 slip, in the 5th space 3 slip = for the 3rd point: in the 5th space, 2 slip, in the 6th space, 5 slip = for the 4th point: in the 6th space 1 slip, in the 7th space 6 slip = for the 5th point: in the 8th space 4 slip, in the 9th space 3 slip = for the 6th point: in the 9th space 3 slip, in the 10th space 4 slip = for the 7th point: in the 11th space 7 slip = for the 8th point: in the 12th space 7 slip = 5 slip in each of the 2 remaining spaces.

Figure 468

Crochet lace

(Fig. 468).—This is an effective pattern in any thread size. It is not new, however, and you may be familiar with it as a pillow lace. Those who are not fond of making pillow lace will be glad to learn how to reproduce it in crochet, for it makes a pretty trimming both for apparel and furniture. For furniture, it should be made in unbleached cotton; for articles of dress, in any of the of the finer threads referred to below.

Materials: For trimming curtains and coarse linen table covers: Fil à pointer DMC No. 25 or 30, or Cordonnet 6 fils DMC Nos. 10 to 25 écru. For articles clothing: Fil d›Alsace DMC Nos. 30 to 70, Cordonnet 6 fils DMC Nos. 25 to 70, or Fil à dentelle DMC Nos. 25 to 70 écru.[A]

For the separate squares, cast on 10 chain stitches and close the ring.

1st row—* 5 chain, 1 slip on the ring. Repeat 3 times from *.

2nd row—1 chain, 1 slip on the first 5 chain: * 5 chain, 1 slip = on the first 5 chain of the 1st row: 2 chain, 1 slip on the second 5 chain of the 1st row. Repeat 3 times from *.

3rd row—1 slip on the first 5 of the 2nd row: * 5 chain, 1 slip, 2 chain,

1 slip, 2 chain, 1 slip. Repeat 3 times from *.

In the **4th and following rows**, go on increasing, as in the 3rd row, until you have 11 slip stitches between every 5 chain on all 4 sides.

12th row—1 slip, 5 chain, 1 slip, * 1 picot made of 4 chain, 1 slip between the 1st and the 2nd slip of the last row, 2 chain, 1 slip between the next 2 slip. Repeat 3 times from * and fasten off.

Crochet the squares together as you finish them. After the 12th and last slip stitch, make 2 chain, drop the loop, put the hook into the 3rd of the 5 chain stitches that form one corner of the square, draw the dropped loop through, 2 chain, close the picot, finish the square.

For the star that connects the squares—10 chain, close the ring; * 4 chain, 1 picot, 4 chain, 1 over, join the 2 picots (right and left of the squares that are to be joined together) by 1 treble; 4 chain, 1 picot, 3 chain, drop the loop, put the needle into the first of the first 4 chain stitches, draw the thread through, 2 slip on the ring, 8 chain, 1 double crochet on the 3rd picot and 1 double crochet on the 4th picot of the square = coming back: 1 slip on each of the 8 chain; 2 slip on the ring, and repeat 3 times from *.

For the half-star that fills the space under the footing of the lace—10 chain, close the ring = 9 chain, 1 double crochet on the 1st picot of the square; 4 chain, 1 picot, 3 chain; draw the thread through the 1st of the 9 chain = 2 slip, 8 chain, join the 3rd and 4th picots of the square by 1 double crochet bar on each picot = 8 single stitches on the 8 chain, 2 slip on the ring; 4 chain, 1 picot, 4 chain = on the 1st and last picot of the 2 opposite squares: 1 treble, 4 chain, 1 picot, 3 chain, drop the loop, draw it through the 1st of the 4 chain stitches = 2 slip, 8 chain, join 2 picots by 2 double crochets = 8 single, 2 slip on the ring, 4 chain, 1 picot, 4 chain, 1 double crochet on the last picot = 8 chain, draw the thread through the 1st of the 4 chain.

The **footing** is made as follows—* 1 slip on the 5 upper chain stitches of the square; 17 chain up to the ring, 3 slip, 17 chain and repeat from *. A row of slip stitches completes the footing.

Outer edge—* 2 double crochet on the 1st picot, 4 chain, and repeat 5 times from *.

On the 5 chain stitches, in the corner, make 1 double crochet = 4 chain, 1 double crochet on the 5 chain, and finish the second side of the square like the first. Omit the chain stitches between the 1st and last double crochets of the squares.

The next and last row consists of 2 slip, 1 picot, 2 slip every 4 chain. On the last 4 chain, at the point where 2 scallops join, make 4 slip stitches without picots.

Figure 469

Lace with stars

(Fig. 469).—Begin with the stars: make a chain of 18 stitches, close the ring, mount it on a mould, wind a soft thread, such as Coton à repriser DMC No 60, seven or eight times round it, and make 30 slip stitches upon it, joining the last to the first by a single stitch.

Materials: Fil d'Alsace DMC Nos. 30 to 70, Fil à pointer DMC No. 25 or 30, Coton pour crochet DMC Nos. 8 to 12.[A]

Then: * 13 chain, and returning, skip the 1st chain = on the 12 chain: 1 single, 2 slip, 2 half double crochets, 2 double crochets, 2 trebles, 1 treble and a half, 2 double trebles; keep the two last loops of the last double crochet but one on the needle, and join them to those of the last treble. Repeat 5 times from *.

2nd row—1 slip, on the upper stitch that was skipped in the 1st row; * 17 chain, 1 slip on the next point. Repeat 5 times from *.

3rd row—* 6 slip, 3 chain, skip 2 stitches of the lower row. Repeat from *.

4th row—All round the last row, on each of the bottom stitches, make 1 slip; after every 6 stitches, 1 picot.

This will give you 19 picots in all, separated from each other by 6 stitches.

Inner connection—Fasten on the thread at the 5th treble, counting from the ring, 1 single, 8 chain. Draw out the thread from the back through the 9th of the 17 chain, round the star = 8 chain * join with 1 chain to the 5th treble, passing the thread through to the back = work on the wrong side: 3 chain, bring the thread back between the 5th double crochet to the right side, and repeat 5 times from *. In joining the stars, place them so that 9 picots are turned to the edge and 8 to the footing. The 10th and 19th picots serve to join the stars.

1st row—2 double crochets between the 19th and the 9th of the * 9 picots, 7 chain, 1 treble; repeat 9 times from *.

After the 10th treble, make no more chain stitches but 1 double crochet immediately between the 19th and 1st picot of the next row.

2nd row—On the 7 first chain stitches of the last row: 3 slip, 4 half double crochets, 3 double crochets, 1 picot, 3 double crochets, 1 picot, and so on, until in the semicircle over the picots you have 7 times 7 chain stitches and 16 picots = on the ninth set of 7 chain: 3 double crochets, 4 half double crochets, 3 slip.

The scallops are joined by smaller ones, formed of 3 slip, 4 half double crochets, 3 double crochets, 1 picot, 2 double crochets, 7 chain, drop the loop, put the needle into the same double crochet of the last scallop; draw the loop through and make on the 7 chain: 1 slip, 1 half double crochet, 5 double crochets, 1 picot, 5 double crochets, 1 half double crochet, 1 slip; continue the large scallop as described above.

The footing is composed of rings and double crochets.—Begin with a ring like those in the middle of the stars, worked as follows: 18 chain with 28 slip upon them = skip 1 slip stitch of the ring, 3 slip, 10 chain = skip 1 slip, 3 slip, 10 chain = skip 1 slip, 3 slip, 5 chain, 1 single on the 7th picot of the 1st star, 5 chain = skip 1 slip, 3 slip, 5 chain, 1 single on the 8th picot, 5 chain = skip 1 slip, 3 slip, 5 chain, 1 single on the 2nd picot, 5 chain, finish off.

Straight edge—Worked from right to left = 1 chain *, turn the thread 7 times round the needle, join to the slip stitch between the 7th and 6th picot, complete the long treble, 7 chain, join 1 treble consisting of six overs to the 1st treble; 1 quadruple treble between the 6th and the 5th picot; 7 chain, 1 triple treble joined to the previous double crochet = in all, 10 double crochets, the 1st made with 7 overs, the 2nd with 6, the 3rd with 5, the 4th with 4, the 5th and 6th with 3, the 7th with 4, the 8th with 5, the 9th with 6, the 10th with 7; and between every 2 double crochets, 7 chain.

The 3 long double crochets of the ring are taken up with 1 slip and 7 chain between.

Figure 470

Guipure lace

(Fig. 470).—We advise our readers to work this charming pattern in unbleached Fil à dentelle DMC No 50, because it imitates the appearance of old lace better than any other material.

Lozenge-shaped figures in the center—5 chain, close the ring.

1st row—5 chain, 1 picot, 2 chain, 1 double crochet on the ring = 5 chain, 1 double crochet on the ring = 2 chain, 1 picot, 2 chain, 1 double crochet on the ring = 5 chain on the 3rd of the first 5 chain.

2nd row—12 chain, * 1 double crochet on the 1st double crochet of the 1st row = 4 chain, 1 double crochet on the 3rd of the next 5 chain = 5 chain, 1 double crochet on the same stitch as the last double crochet = 4 chain, ** 1 double crochet on the 2nd double crochet of the 1st row, 9 chain. Repeat from * to **; join the last 4 chain, to the 3rd of the first 12 chain, by a single stitch.

3rd row—1 chain, 4 slip, 3 slip on the 5th of the 9 chain of the last row = 12 slip, 5 slip on the 3rd of the 5 chain, between the 2 double crochets, 12 slip, 3 slip on the 5th of the lower 9 chain = 12 slip, 5 slip on the 3rd of the 5 chain, 7 slip; finish the row with a single stitch.

4th row—3 chain, 1 double crochet on each of the next 5 slip; 3 double crochets on the 6th slip; 1 double crochet on each of the next 15 slip, 5 double crochets on the 16th stitch; 15 double crochets on the 2nd side; and again 3 double crochets on the 16th stitch; 15 double crochets on the 3rd side; 5 double crochets on the 16th stitch, 9 double crochets and join to the 3rd of the 3 chain.

5th row—1 chain, 6 slip, 3 slip on the 7th stitch beneath, * 18 slip, 3 slip on the 19th stitch. Repeat twice from *.

6th row—1 chain, 1 picot, 2 slip, 1 picot, 2 slip, 1 picot = toward the point: 3 slip, 1 picot = on the 2nd side of the square: 3 slip, 1 picot, and 5 times 2 slip, 1 picot = toward the point: 4 slip, 1 picot.

On the 3rd side as on the 2nd, except reversed, make first 4 slip, and at the point, 3 slip. Make the 4th side as on the 2nd; on the 1st side must still be added 3 slip, 1 picot, 2 slip, 1 picot, 2 slip, 1 picot, 2 slip; draw the thread through the loop and fasten off.

The oblong squares that connect the lozenges take 7 rows of slip stitches. Make a chain of 14 = turn the work = 13 slip; add 5 rows of the same number of stitches. On the short side, and at the edge of the square: 1 picot, 3 slip, * 9 chain, skip 1 chain = returning: 1 slip on the 8th chain = on the next 7 chain: 1 half double crochet, 3 double crochets, 1 half double crochet, 2 slip on the last chain stitches = on the 2nd half of the short side: 3 slip, 1 picot = on the long side: 3 slip **, 1 picot, 3 slip ***. Repeat the whole twice from * to ***, and then once from * to ** only.

The row of bars that encircles the small leaves begins with 2 single stitches on the first picot, then add: **** 3 chain, 1 picot, 3 chain, 1 double crochet on the 9th chain of the small leaf; on the short side: 1 chain, 1 picot, 1 chain, 1 double treble on the 9th chain of the leaf; drop the thread, bring it out from the back by the side of the picot that forms the corner on the long side of the lozenge = 1 chain, 1 picot, 1 chain, 1 double crochet on the small leaf = 3 chain, 1 picot, 3 chain, 1 double crochet on the picot, forming the corner of the oblong square = 3 chain, 1 picot, 3 chain, 1 double crochet on the leaf on the long side of the square = 3 chain, 1 double crochet on the same stitch as the 1st double crochet is on = 3 chain, 1 double crochet on the same stitch as the first 2 double crochets are on; 3 chain, 1 picot, 3 chain, 1 double crochet on the picot at the corner. Repeat once from ****.

Upper and lower edge—6 chain, 1 quintuple treble on the 2nd picot of the lozenge = 6 chain, 1 double treble on the 4th picot of the lozenge. Coming back over the 2 double crochets of 6 chain work in 3 journeys to and fro, 13 slip stitches.

After the 2nd row of slip stitches, 1 quadruple treble on the 6th double crochet of the lozenge, and then 4 rows of slip stitches.

After the 6th row, pass at once to the leaves above the lozenge: ***** 15 chain, 1 slip on the picot that forms the point of the lozenge = turn the work to the wrong side = on the chain stitches, work: ****** 3 slip, 1 half double crochet, 4 double crochets, 1 half double crochet, 3 slip = turn the work to the right side = returning and starting from the point of the leaf: 1 chain and 1 slip on each of the lower stitches.

For the 2nd leaf: 12 chain = turn the work and repeat, as for the former leaf, from ***** to ******.

This leaf will be finished like the first, except that it will end at the upper point. Pass to the 2nd little square: 6 chain, 1 quintuple treble on the picot next to the leaves; 3 chain, 1 double treble on the 3rd picot, counted from the leaves = 6 chain, 1 quintuple treble on the 5th picot of the lozenge; keep the 2 last loops of the double crochet on the needle, 1 quintuple treble on the picot between every 3 chain of the small square with leaves; draw up the 2 last loops together with those already on the needle = 6 chain, 1 double treble on the picot on the long side of the small square = 3 rows of 13 slip each.

With the last stitch of each of these rows, take 1 of the chain stitches between the long double crochets.

After the 3rd row: 1 quintuple treble on the first double crochet on the small leaf of the small middle square = 3 rows of slip stitches to finish the square, and repeat from *****.

The upper row is similar to this but should be worked from right to left.

Scalloped edge—In the right corner of the 1st oblong figure of the outside corner: 1 treble, 2 chain, 1 treble on the 4th slip stitch = 2 chain, 1 treble on the stitch that forms the corner stitch of the square = 2 chain, 1 slip at the extremity of the first long leaf, 9 chain = 1 triple treble on the stitch between the 2 leaves = 2 chain, 1 triple treble on the same stitch and on the 1st double crochet = 2 chain, 1 triple treble on the same stitch = 9 chain, 1 slip on the last stitch of the 2nd long leaf = turn the work: 1 chain, 1 slip on each of the chain stitches, and on each treble, 27 slip stitches in all = turn the work: 1 chain, 1 slip, 2 chain, 1 slip on the 2nd slip; repeat the last 12 times. Take in 1 stitch on each side in every row, turn the work after each row, and at the end of the last, fasten off. Fasten on at the foot of the scallop, not at the point, and work slip stitches all around it; 20 slip to the upper point, 40 in all.

The open-work edge of the scallops consists entirely of trebles.—After the 40 slip stitches of the edge: 2 chain, 1 double crochet on the 1st slip stitch of the small square = turn the work: * 2 chain, 1 double crochet on the 2nd of the slip stitches, forming the edge of the scallop **; repeat 7 times from * to ** = *** 2 chain, 1 double crochet on the next slip stitch = 2 chain, 1 double crochet on the next slip = repeat 4 times from ***; and then 7 times from * to ** = 2 chain, 1 slip on the 4th double crochet of the square; 2 chain, 1 slip on the 3rd treble.

Work on, on the right side = **** 2 chain and 1 double crochet on the preceding double crochet as far as the 8th treble; after the 8th: ***** 10 chain, back to the 7th, and returning, join to the 7th double crochet = on the 10 chain: 16 slip, after the 16th draw the loop through the upper loop of the 8th double crochet = ****** 2 chain, 1 treble, 2 chain, 1 treble, 10 chain, return, and fasten the chain stitches to the last double crochet but one = 6 slip, 1 picot, 2 slip, 1 picot, 6 slip and join as before ******* = Repeat once from ***** to *******, then twice, from ***** to ******, then from **** to *****, as on the first side, only 1 double crochet less = then 1 double crochet on the 4th slip stitch of the small square, 2 chain, 1 double crochet on the 7th slip stitch of the square, 2 chain, 1 double crochet on the 10th slip stitch, 1 double crochet on the outside stitch, at the corner of the square, 2 chain, 1 slip on the last stitch of the leaf; 9 chain and so on, as above described.

Having reached the second scallop, on the 2nd row of double crochets, at the sign ***, work 2 chain, 1 double crochet to the left on the scallop just finished, keeping the last loops of the double crochet on the needle, 1 treble to the right of the scallop and join it to the 2nd treble; draw the 4 loops together = 2 chain, 1 double crochet to the left, 1 triple treble to the right = 11 chain, drop the loop, bring it to the right side through the 4th double crochet of the right scallop = on these, 11 chain stitches: 1 single, 1 slip, 1 half double crochet, 2 double crochets, 1 half double crochet, 1 slip, 1 single = 1 treble on the open-work edge, then 2 chain, 1 treble, 2 chain, 1 treble, 12 chain; join to the 6th double crochet of the right scallop = working back: 4 slip, 1 picot, 4 slip, 1 picot, 4 slip, 1 picot, 4 slip, join to the treble, thrice 2 chain, 1 treble. Go back to ***** and repeat twice to *******.

The footing of the lace is worked in 5 rows from right to left.

1st row—1 single, * 1 treble on the 6th slip stitch of the square = 1 chain, 1 treble on the 2nd slip stitch of the square = 3 chain, 1 picot downward, 3 chain, 1 slip on the stitch at the extremity of the long leaf = 3 chain, 1 picot downward, 3 chain, 2 triple trebles between the two leaves = 3 chain, 1 picot downward, 3 chain, 1 slip on the last stitch of the 2nd leaf, 3 chain; repeat from *.

2nd row—1 slip on each stitch of the previous row.

3rd row—count 2 stitches before and above the 2 double crochets on the squares and make: * 1 treble, skip 1 stitch, 1 treble, skip 1 stitch, 1 treble, skip 1 stitch, 1 double crochet = turn the work: 1 slip on each of the 4 double crochets = turn the work, come back and make 4 slip on the first 4 = 5 chain, skip 2 stitches of the 2nd row, 1 double crochet on the 3rd slip, and continue from *.

4th row—1 double crochet on each of the 4 slip, 1 chain between each treble, 2 chain and so on.

5th row—1 slip stitch on each of the stitches of the 4th row.

Figure 471

Crochet Reticella lace

(Fig. 471).—This pattern, copied in crochet from an old piece of Reticella lace, only looks good worked in very fine cotton, as indicated in the illustration. We recommend unbleached Fil à dentelle DMC No 150. To make the work resemble the original more closely, the method adopted in Venetian point of making all the stitches over a padding thread on the outside edge, been followed here.

At the end of each row of slip stitches, draw out a sufficiently long loop to lay back over the stitches just made. Work the next row of stitches over this double foundation. These loops must be long enough not to pucker or tighten the scallops.

For the inner squares = 4 chain, close the ring.

1st row—8 chain, 1 treble, 3 chain, 1 treble, 3 chain, 1 treble, 3 chain, 1 treble, 3 chain, 1 treble, 3 chain, 1 treble, 3 chain, 1 treble, 3 chain, 1 single stitch on the 5th of the 8 chain.

2nd row—* 1 chain, 5 slip on the first 3 chain, 5 slip on the next 3 chain. On these 10 slip stitches, working to and fro, 9 rows of slip stitches, decreasing by 1 in each row; after the last stitch, come back along the side of the little triangle and make 1 single stitch in every row, 1 slip on the double crochet of the 1st row **; repeat 3 times from * to **.

These small triangles must be worked over 1 double crochet and between 2 trebles.

When the 4th triangle is finished, start from the last stitch at the point along the side and make 3 slip, 1 picot, 3 slip, 1 picot, 3 slip; 1 single stitch on the treble; all the triangles must be edged, in this same manner on both sides; on the stitch that forms the point: 3 slip stitches.

3rd row—* 17 chain, drop the loop = bring it to the front through the slip stitch that lies between 2 triangles; returning, make 10 single stitches backward on the 10 chain. You will make stitches like this, backward, in all the double crochets that follow, that is, the loop is dropped after each stitch, and brought forward from the wrong side to the right = 13 chain, join to the 5th single, counting upward from below = 7 single on the chain stitches; 13 chain, join to the other double crochets; 6 chain, 1 single on the stitch at the point of the triangle **; repeat 3 times from * to **. = The chain stitches for the double crochets must be drawn up very tight.

4th row—1 slip on each of the stitches of the preceding row, 3 slip on the corner stitch. On each side, there must be 29 slip stitches, not counting the corner ones.

5th row = 6 chain, skip 2 stitches of the row beneath, * 1 treble, 2 chain; repeat 3 times from * = 2 chain, 1 treble, 2 chain, 1 treble on the same stitch as the 1st double crochet = 2 chain, 1 treble on the same stitch as the 1st double crochet = 2 chain, 1 treble on the same stitch as the two first double crochets = 10 times to the next corner: 2 chain, 1 treble, 3 trebles, each of them with 2 chain stitches at the corner; repeat the same on each of the 4 sides.

6th row—1 slip on each of the stitches of the last row, 3 slip on the corner stitch = cut off the thread. Join the next squares together by the last corner stitch.

Lower edge—Begin by making a large scallop at the point of the square, and pass the double thread over the 3rd double crochet that comes before the 3 double crochets at the point of the square. Make 1 slip stitch on each stitch of the square, up to the 3rd double crochet on the opposite side; then draw out a long loop which you carry back to the beginning. In the 2nd row, increase by 2 stitches, right and left of the middle stitches, for the rounding of the scallop, and decrease by 1 on each side. Make 10 rows in all, and in each row, decrease by 4 stitches and increase by 2. Fasten off after the 10th row.

The two little scallops right and left of the big one are worked in 5 rows over 5 double crochets and 4 intervals of chain stitches, taking off 2 stitches in every row. For the small triangle between, worked in 4 rows, you must increase on both sides by 2 stitches.

When all the scallops are finished, edge them with 3 slip stitches, 1 picot and 3 slip and work in all the ends of thread from the preceding rows at the same time.

For the footing and the small triangles that fill up the spaces between the squares, 22 chain, skip 1, 10 rows of slip stitches, worked back and forth, decreasing by 1 in every row.

When the triangle is finished, make 1 single in every row on one side; then, on the 11 remaining chain stitches, make a second triangle like the first. Then join it to the slip stitches above the 5th treble; then, returning along the side of the triangle, add 3 slip, 1 picot, 3 slip, 1 picot, 3 slip; 1 single on each of the 22 chain stitches.

Edge the next side of the 2nd triangle like the first, join the corner stitch to the 5th treble; edge the two inner sides 3 times with 3 slip stitches and 2 picots.

Then from right to left on the slip stitches: 6 slip, 15 chain, join them to the middle of the 2 triangles = 1 single on each chain, 5 slip on the square; 11 chain, 1 single on the 9th of the first 15 chain; 1 single stitch on each of the chain stitches; 1 slip on each stitch of the square, to the point where the squares join, 8 chain, 1 single on the 6th of the 11 chain, 1 single on each of the 8 chain.

On the 2nd side: 7 slip, 5 chain, 1 single on the 6th of the 11 chain, 1 single on each of the 5 chain, 5 slip, 9 chain, 1 single on the 9th of the 15 chain, 1 single on each of the 9 chain, 6 slip on the square; fasten off.

Fasten on, at the 2nd of the 3 corner stitches = 17 chain, 1 slip on the corner stitch of the triangle; 8 chain, 1 slip on the next corner stitch, 17 chain, and so on.

A row of slip stitches, or double crochets, completes the lace.

Figure 472

Lace with corner, formed by increasing on the outside

(Fig. 472).—**1st row**—On a row of chain stitches or double crochets, work alternately 1 chain, 1 double crochet = on the corner: 1 chain, 1 treble, 2 chain, so that the last 3 double crochets come on one stitch.

2nd row—1 slip on each stitch of the 1st row, 3 slip on the 2nd of the 3 corner double crochets.

3rd row—Counting toward the left from the 2nd of the 3 corner stitches, make 1 slip on the 53rd, 52nd, 51st and 50th slip stitches; 8 chain, skip 1 chain, 1 slip on each of the 7 chain stitches = on the other side of the 8 chain, also 1 slip on each stitch, 3 slip on the 8th chain, 1 slip on each of the first 7 slip.

On the next 11 stitches of the 2nd row: 1 slip = 4 chain, skip 4, 1 double treble on the 5th of the 2nd row, 4 chain, 1 double treble on the same stitch, 4 chain, 1 double treble on the same stitch, 4 chain, skip 4, 1 single on the 5th = turn the work = on each double crochet of 4 chain: 7 slip; 28 in all; 1 single on the 10th of the

11 slip = turn the work = skip the 28th slip, and on the 27 others make: 3 slip, 1 picot, 3 slip = 11 chain, skip the 11th, 10 slip on the others = on the 2nd side of the chain: 4 slip, 10 chain, join them to the 6th of the first 11 slip of this row = on the 10 chain: 5 slip, 3 chain, join them to the 5th slip of the 1st leaf, made in this row = on the 3 chain: 3 slip = on those of the 10 remaining chain stitches: 6 slip = along the leaf: 3 slip, 1 picot, 3 slip = on the stitch at the point of the leaf: 3 slip = then down the 2nd side: 3 slip, 1 picot, 7 slip = over the next of the 28 slip: 3 slip, 1 picot, 4 slip = * 11 chain, skip the 11th, 10 slip = on the second side of the chain: 4 slip, 6 chain, join them to the 4th of the last 7 slip of the 2nd leaf = on the 6 chain: 9 slip. Continue on the 3rd leaf of this row: 3 slip, 1 picot, 3 slip and 3 slip on the stitch at the point of the leaf = on each of the next 3 stitches: 1 slip, then 1 picot, 7 slip = on the 28 stitches: 4 slip, 1 picot, 3 slip **. Repeat from * to **, and here follow: 3 slip, 1 picot, 3 slip.

On the **2nd row**: *** 5 slip, 10 chain, join them to the 4th of the last 7 slip of the 3rd leaf; 11 slip over the 10 chain = on the 2nd row: 5 slip, 8 chain, skip 1 chain, 1 slip on each chain = on the second side: 4 slip, 3 chain, join them to the 6th of the last 11 slip = 3 slip on the leaf, 3 slip on the stitch at the point, 7 slip, and repeat from *.

On the 2nd row and for the corner: 9 slip, **** 4 chain, 1 double treble on the 2nd of the 3 corner stitches and repeat 4 times from **** = 4 chain, skip 4 of the preceding row, 1 slip on the 5th = turn the work, on each bar of 4 chain, 6 slip, 36 in all, join the last to the 8th of the 9 slip = going back over the 36 slip: 3 slip, 1 picot, 3 slip, 11 chain, skip the 11th, 1 slip on each of the 10 chain = on the 2nd side of the chain: 4 slip, 10 chain, join them to the 4th of the 9 slip = over the 10 chain: 5 slip, 3 chain, join them to the 4th slip of the last leaf, 3 slip = on the remainder of the 10 chain: 6 slip.

Proceeding along the leaf: 3 slip, 1 picot, 3 slip, 3 slip on the stitch at the point, 3 slip, 1 picot, 7 slip *****. Again on the 36 slip, make: 3 slip, 1 picot, 3 slip, 11 chain, skip the 11th, 10 slip = on the 2nd side of the chain: 4 slip, 6 chain, join them to the 4th of the last 7 slip of the last leaf, 9 slip over the chain stitches = on the leaf: 3 slip, 1 picot, 3 slip, 3 slip on the stitch at the point, 3 slip, 1 picot, 7 slip ******. Repeat 3 times from ***** to ****** and add 3 slip, 1 picot, 3 slip. Continue along the 2nd row: 4 slip, 10 chain and on these 11 slip = 4 slip, 8 chain, returning, skip the 8th, 7 slip on the others = on the 2nd side of the chain: 4 slip, 3 chain, join them to the 6th of the last 11 slip = on the 3 chain: 3 slip = on the leaf: 3 slip, 3 slip on the stitch at the point of the leaf, 7 slip.

4th row—1 slip on the 1st leaf of the 3rd row: * 7 chain, 1 slip on the 2nd leaf = 7 chain, 1 double treble on the 5th of the 9 slip between 2 leaves = 7 chain, 1 slip on the 3rd leaf = 7 chain, 1 double treble, 7 chain, 1 slip on the 4th leaf = 7 chain, 1 slip on the 5th leaf; 5 chain, 1 slip on the 1st leaf of the corner scallop. Repeat from *, with this difference: in the corner scallop, make 4 double trebles.

5th row—on the first 7 chain of the 4th row: 7 slip, * on the next chain stitches: 12 slip = turn the work, and crochet to and fro, decreasing by 1 stitch in each row, until you have only 2 stitches left = along the leaf: 10 slip and repeat 3 times from * = 7 slip on the next 7 chain, 6 slip on the 5 chain, 7 slip on the 7 chain.

The corner scallop has 7 points = the 12 first stitches must be divided as follows: * 1st point: 12 slip in the first interval = 2nd point: 10 slip in the 2nd interval and 2 slip in the 3rd interval = 3rd point: 7 slip in the 3rd interval and 5 slip in the 4th **. Repeat once from ** to *.

6th row—* 1 slip in the 1st leaf, 5 chain, 1 crossed triple treble, the branches of which are joined by 5 chain; repeat twice from * = 1 slip, 4 chain, 1 slip in the 1st leaf of the next scallop = 5 chain, 1 crossed triple treble, the branches of which are joined by 5 chain and joined to the 6th stitch of the 2 next points = 5 chain and so on.

7th row—6 slip on the first 5 chain of the 6th row, 6 slip on the next chain = 8 chain; carry the chain back to the right, and join it on, between the 6th and 7th slip = 4 slip on the 8 chain, then 8 chain, take it back, and join to the 1st slip = 12 slip on the 8 chain = continue on the small scallop: 3 slip, 1 picot, 8 slip = on the other 5 chain: 6 slip = 8 chain, join them again to the 4th of the 8 slip on the scallop = on the last 8 chain: 3 slip, 1 picot, 8 slip = on the 2 next bars of 5 chain: 12 slip = 8 chain, join them to the 7th of the last 12 slip = on the 8 chain: 5 slip = 8 chain, join them to the 1st of the last 12 slip = on the 8 chain: 5 slip, 3 chain, join them to the 4th slip of the 3rd finished scallop = over the 3 chain: 2 slip, 1 picot, 2 slip = on the next scallop: 3 slip, 1 picot, 3 slip = in the half finished scallop: 6 slip = 8 chain, take it back and join it to the 1st of the last 6 slip = on the 8 chain: 5 slip, 1 picot, 3 slip, 1 picot, 5 slip to finish the scallop below: 5 slip = on the 6th row: 6 slip, 8 chain, join them to the first of the last 5 slip of the last scallop = on the 8 chain: 3 slip, 1 picot, 8 slip.

The little scallops must continue around the corner point as they were on the 3rd, 4th, and 5th double crochets of the other points.

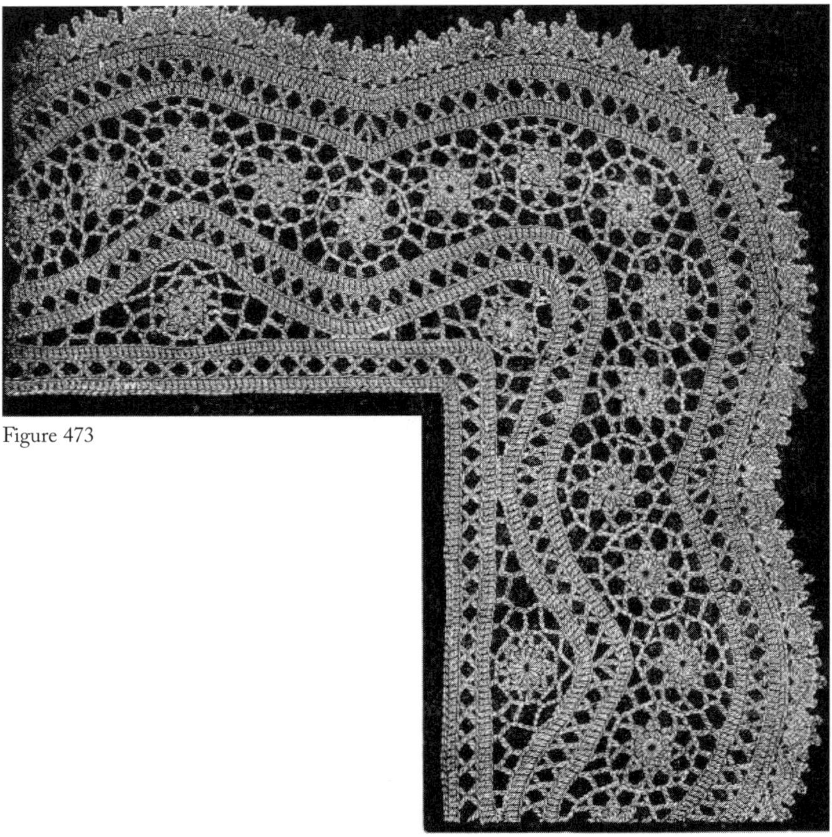

Figure 473

Lace with corner, formed by decreasing on the inside

(Fig. 473).—For the stars—8 chain, close the ring; 3 chain, 15 double crochets in the ring; close = 3 chain, skip 1 double crochet of the last row, 1 treble, 5 chain, 1 double crochet on the upper part of the last double crochet = alternate 7 times: 1 chain, 1 crossed double crochet divided by 2 chain, lastly 1 chain, close the ring, fasten off.

Materials: Fil d'Alsace DMC Nos. 30 to 70, Fil à pointer DMC No. 20 or 30, Coton pour crochet DMC Nos. 10 to 18, or Cordonnet 6 fils DMC Nos. 4 to 60.[A] Colors: White, Écru naturel or any other color of the 450 shades of the DMC color card.

Make 11 stars and join them together as follows: counting the third from the left in the engraving, as the first. When you have joined the 1st star to the 2nd by the 6th and 7th cross double crochets, join the next stars so that when the 3rd is fastened on, there are 2 crossed double crochets on the inside and outside of the 2nd star. The 3rd star will have 1 crossed double crochet on the outside, 3 on the inside = the 4th: 2 crossed double crochets inside, 2 outside = the 5th, the 6th, and the 7th: 1 inside, 3 outside = the 8th: 2 on the inside and outside = the 9th: 3 inside, 1 outside = the 10th: 2 outside, 2 inside = the 11th: 3 outside, 1 inside. For the next scallops, repeat from the 2nd to the 5th star.

2nd row—* over the 2 chain stitches of the 3rd crossed double crochet of the 11th star: 1 treble, 3 chain = over the 1st chain stitch between the 3rd and 4th crossed double crochets: 1 treble, 3 chain = over the next 2 chain stitches: 1 treble, 3 chain = 3 overs, in the next space: 1 treble and 1 treble in the 1st space of the 10th star; connect the two double crochets together, 3 chain, 1 treble, 3 chain, 1 treble, 3 chain, 1 treble, 3 chain, 1 connected double crochet as before, 3 chain ** 1 slip over the 2 chain stitches of the last crossed double crochet of the 9th star. Repeat from ** to *, therefore backward.

Each of the next double crochets comes, either over 2 chain stitches of the crossed treble, or over the chain stitch between the crossed double crochets *** 3 chain, 1 treble, 3 chain, 1 treble, 3 chain, 1 triple connected treble, 3 chain, 1 treble, 3 chain, 1 treble, 3 chain **** 1 single; repeat, in the reverse order, from **** to ***.

When the outside row is finished, make a similar row on the inside of the stars; at the corner, 3 double crochets are to be made 3 times over each of the middle stars.

3rd row—1 double crochet above and below on each stitch of the second row.

4th row—consists entirely of crossed double crochets = * skip on the upper edge: 3 times 1 treble and 5 times 2 double crochets = on the next double crochets of the preceding row: 1 treble, skip 2 stitches, 1 treble, skip 2 stitches, 1 treble = draw up the last loops of the 3 double crochets together = repeat the same thing backward = here follow: 8 crossed double crochets separated each by 1 double crochet of the preceding row **; the 8th and the 9th crossed double crochets are together in the corner double crochet of the preceding row. Repeat from ** to * = follow 1 row with 1 double crochet on every stitch below.

The row on the side of the footing is worked as described = at the corner, and after having made the 3rd connected treble, * skip 5 times 2 stitches, 6 times 1 stitch, 3 times 2 stitches, 3 times 3 stitches, ** 3 double trebles connected together above, skip 3 stitches underneath; repeat from ** to *, followed on both sides by a row of double crochets.

In the corner of the inside row of double crochets, connect the loops of 5 pairs of double crochets, in the center connect the loops of 3 double crochets and then again the loops of 5 pairs of double crochets.

For the 1st star of the footing: 8 chain, close the ring; 3 chain in the ring, 15 double crochets, close = 3 chain, skip 1 treble, 1 treble, * 3 chain, 1 double crochet on the stitch of the 1st treble, skip 1, 1 double crochet in the 2nd stitch, draw the loops of the 2 double crochets together **. Repeat 6 times from * to **; add 3 chain and close = 5 chain, join them to the 15th double crochet of the last row; 5 chain, 1 slip on the first chain stitches between 2 double crochets; 4 chain, join them to the 7th treble; 4 chain, 1 slip on the next chain stitches, 3 chain, join to the double crochet over the 3 connected double trebles, 3 chain, 1 slip on the next chain stitches, 4 chain, join them to the 8th treble, 5 chain, 1 slip on the 5th treble, cut off the thread.

The corner star is made like the one just described and is joined on as follows: 3 chain, join them to the 17th double crochet on the left of the last row (counting from the double treble) = 3 chain, 1 slip on the first chain stitches between 2 double crochets = 3 chain, skip 4 double crochets, join them to the 5th = 3 chain, 1 slip on the 2nd set of chain stitches between = 6 chain, skip 5 double crochets, join them to the 6th = 3 chain, 1 slip on the 3rd of the 6 last chain = 3 chain, join them to the corner stitch, 3 chain, 1 slip on the last 3 chain = toward the right: 3 chain, join to the 5th double crochet = 3 chain, 1 slip on the preceding, 3 chain, 1 slip on the 3rd set of stitches between, 3 chain, skip 4 double crochets, join to the 5th double crochet = 3 chain, 1 slip on the 4th set of stitches between, 3 chain, skip 4 stitches and join = 3 chain, 1 slip on the 5th treble, fasten off.

On the 3 first double crochets of the preceding row of the inside edge, counting from the outermost stitches which are to be seen to the right in the illustration, 1 slip, 3 chain, skip 4 double crochets, 1 double crochet = 3 chain, skip 3 double crochets, 1 treble, 3 chain, 3 overs, pass the needle over the treble, crochet off one over = skip 3 stitches, 1 treble, crochet off the 2 remaining loops = 3 chain, 4 overs, crochet off 2 loops, 1 treble over the chain double crochet of the star, crochet off the remaining loops = 3 chain, 3 overs over the double crochet made on the 5 chain, crochet off 2 loops = 1 double crochet on the 5th set of stitches between, crochet off the remaining loops = 3 chain, 1 double crochet on the 6th set of stitches between = 3 chain, 1 double crochet on the 7th set of stitches between = 3 chain, 3 overs, 1 double crochet on the 8th set of stitches between; crochet off 1 over, 1 treble on the 5 first chain stitches of the star, crochet off the remaining loops = 3 chain, 3 overs, 1 double crochet over the 2nd treble, 1 treble, skip 2 double crochets of the preceding row, complete the double crochet = 3 chain, 3 overs, crochet off 1 over, joining it to the last treble; crochet off the overs = 1 double crochet on the 5th double crochet of the preceding row, crochet off the loops = 3 chain, 1 double crochet on the 4th double crochet = 3 chain, skip 4 stitches = on each of the 6 following double crochets: 1 slip = 3 chain, skip 3 double crochets, 1 treble, 3 chain, skip 3 double crochets, 1 treble; 3 chain, 3 overs, over the treble crochet off 1 loop, 1 treble on the 4th double crochet after the slip stitches, crochet off the last overs = 3 chain, 3 overs, over the last treble crochet off 1 loop, 1 treble on the 5th intervening space of the corner star, crochet off the loops = 3 chain, 1 slip on the 7th treble of the star = 3 chain, 1 treble on the 8th intervening space = 3 chain, 3 overs, over the last treble crochet off 2 loops, 1 treble on the 3rd double crochet of the preceding row, complete the double crochet = 3 chain, 3 overs, over the treble crochet off 2 loops, 1 double crochet on the 4th treble, complete the double crochet = 3 chain, 1 double crochet on the 4th treble, 3 chain, skip 3, 3 slip.

To finish with one row of double crochets, draw the 5 corner double crochets together and add 1 row of crossed double crochets and 1 row of slip double crochets, each time drawing the 5 corner loops together into one.

1st row of the outside border—1 slip on every one of the next 7 double crochets of the row beneath, 5 chain; turn back, join them to the 7th slip, and so on.

2nd row—1 slip on the 4th of the 7 slip, 9 double crochets on the 5 chain.

3rd row—1 slip on each of the first 2 double crochets of the 2nd row, 1 picot, 2 slip, 1 picot, skip 1 stitch, 2 slip, 1 picot, 2 slip, and so on.

Figure 474

Square with colored tufts

(Fig. 474).—The following are different counterpane patterns which should be worked in coarse cotton; our engraving represents a single square worked in two colors in raised crochet. By joining a number of such squares together, 4 or 6 colors can be used in one covering with very good effect.

Materials: Coton pour crochet DMC Nos. 6 to 10, or Coton à tricoter DMC Nos. 6 to 12.[A] Colors. White and Rouge-Turc 321, or écru and Bleu-Indigo 321, Rouge-Géranium 353 and Brun-Caroubier 356, Bleu d›Azur 3325 and Brun-Rouille 3312, Vert-Bouteille 494 and Bleu-Prunelle 489.[A]

Cast on 13 chain and close the ring.

1st row—1 slip on the 1st of the 13 chain, 5 chain, 1 slip on the 4th chain, 5 chain, 1 slip on the 7th chain, 5 chain, 1 slip on the 10th chain, 5 chain, 1 slip on the 13th chain.

2nd row—1 slip on the 1st slip of the 1st row, * 1 slip on the 1st of the 5 chain; 5 chain, 1 slip on the 5th chain. Repeat 3 times from *.

3rd row—5 slip on the 5 chain, 5 chain, 5 slip and so on.

4th and 5th rows—continue to increase, as in the 3rd row.

6th row—after the 3rd slip, make 1 tuft in the contrasting color (see fig. 431).

The contrasting color is to be introduced into the work at the first tuft and cut off when the last is finished.

The ends of the colored threads must be worked in under the stitches of the next row. The square may be any size; it is bordered by small picot scallops which join the different squares.

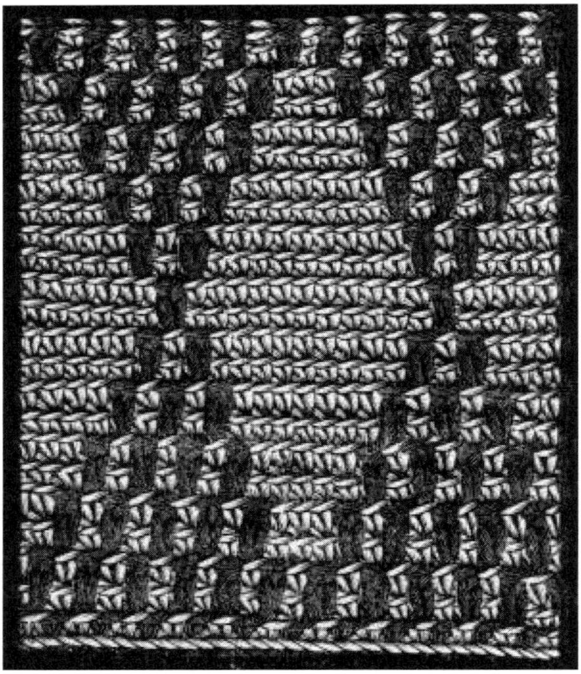

Figure 475

Stripes for counterpanes

(Fig. 475).—We recommend the use of Soutache DMC or Lacets superfins DMC (braids) for the colored stitches, in the place of cotton. The pattern will look brighter if the dark stitches are worked on a lighter background and in a flat material that will spread out more than cotton does.

The stripe, worked in its entire length and always on the right side, must be begun by a chain of stitches of the length the stripe is to be.

Materials: Coton pour crochet DMC Nos. 6 to 8, or Coton à tricoter DMC Nos. 6 to 12 and Lacets surfins DMC No. 4, or Soutache DMC No. 2½.[A] Colors: Gris-Lin 716 and Rouge-Bordeaux 497, Gris-Tilleul 393 and Bleu-Faience 484 or Brun-Caroubier 356 and Jaune-Rouille 308 etc.[A]

1st row—1 slip stitch on each chain stitch.

2nd row—1 slip stitch with white or unbleached cotton on each second stitch of the preceding row; 1 long slip stitch with the colored cotton or the braid in each second loop of the chain stitch.

When red and white cotton are used, only one thread must be drawn through the 1st loop; the other goes through the last two loops.

3rd, 5th, 7th, 9th, 11th rows—slip stitches of the color of the grounding = 4th row—between every 5 colored stitches 3 white = 6th row—between every 4 red, 5 white = 8th row—between every 3 red, 7 white = 10th row—between every 2 red, 9 white = 12th row—between the single red stitches, 11 white slip.

In the second half of the pattern, the red stitches must increase at the same rate that they decreased before.

Figure 476

Pattern of a counterpane in Tunisian crochet

(Fig. 476). This pattern of a counterpane in Tunisian crochet, though it is worked here in several colors, can be done all in one. The numbers of the stitches, as they are given here, refer to the pattern represented in our figure; if worked on a larger scale, the number of stitches would have to be increased by the proper proportion.

For the inner square, which is worked in a light material, make 20 chain stitches. On these stitches, make 17 rows of plaited Tunisian crochet, fig. 445, then fasten off.

Materials: Coton pour crochet DMC Nos. 6 to 8, or Coton à tricoter DMC Nos. 6 to 12.[A] Colors: Gris-Amadou 385 and Rouge-Cardinal 346, Vert-Bouteille 492 and Violet-Mauve 316, or Bleu-Gentiane 479 and Gris-Écru 706.

For the first colored border, which immediately surrounds the center square, take a colored thread and make 2 chain stitches. On these stitches, make the common Tunisian stitch, fig. 444. Increase to the right in every row by one stitch, to the number of 6 = then put the needle into the first stitch on one side of the square, turn the thread round, and draw it through. Here you must be careful to observe that the second part which is now to be joined to the square should always remain on the left side of the square and that the thread with which you join the two parts together should lie to the left and be drawn through from the wrong side to the right. Having now got 7 Tunisian stitches on the needle, make 18 double rows and join the last stitch of each row to a stitch of the square.

When these rows are finished, proceed to decrease on the right until you have only 2 stitches left; then increase as at the beginning of the stripe. At each increase, after each double row, you must pass the thread through the corresponding stitch opposite the same row. When you have 7 stitches on the needle, join them as before to the square. Work around the 4 sides of the square in this manner, and when you come to the last decrease, join the stitches to those of the first increase and fasten off. The next stripes are to be worked in the same way; they may be made either wider or narrower, and either plain or ornamented with a cross stitch pattern.

Figure 477

Pattern of counterpane worked in stripes

(Fig. 477).—This is intended for a child's coverlet and is worked in pale blue, Bleu-Indigo 334, and white; the stripes and the lace border, in white; the setting, partly in white, partly in blue.

Materials: Coton pour crochet DMC Nos. 6 to 12, Coton à tricoter DMC Nos. 6 to 14, or Cordonnet 6 fils DMC No. 15.[A]

For the first stripe, make a foundation chain of 26 stitches; then counting back, draw the needle through the 6th and 7th chain stitches, drawing up all the three loops together = 2 chain, then put the needle again through 2 chain stitches, draw up the 3 loops together = 2 chain and so on.

Coming back, make the loops of the first second stitches on the chain stitches of the preceding row = begin every row with 3 chain, which form picots along the edge of the stripe; when the stripes are finished, take a blue thread and make 1 slip stitch on each picot and 3 chain.

This blue row is followed by a white one, worked in cluster stitch, fig. 426, with 2 chain stitches between every 2 clusters.

Then follows another blue row of one slip stitch on each chain stitch of the previous row. The second blue row consists entirely of slip stitches worked along the long sides of the stripes, which are joined together afterward, but not along the short sides until the counterpane is finished; then the stitches should border all 4 sides. The second stripe, which should be of the same width as the first, is worked in Tunisian crochet; for the edge make one row of slip stitches in blue, one of cluster stitches in white, and then again a row of slip in blue.

Join the stripes with slip stitches on the wrong side, taking up one loop on the right and one on the left, alternately.

When you have joined the stripes, make the outer border, which consists of 7 straight rows and a scalloped lace edging.

1st row—in blue: 3 chain and 1 slip on each picot, 1 slip, and so on, down the long sides of the stripes = along the short sides, the side of the chain stitches or that of the previous row: 1 slip, 3 chain, skip 2, 1 slip.

2nd row—in white or unbleached: 1 cluster stitch, fig. 426, on each picot formed by the 3 chain stitches of the 1st row; on the corner picots, you must make 3 cluster stitches.

3rd, 4th, 5th rows—in blue: similar to the first. Increase at the corners by making: 1 slip, 3 chain, 1 slip on the same stitch.

6th row—in white or unbleached: similar to the 2nd row.

7th row—in blue: 1 double crochet on each of the stitches of the previous row.

Lace edging—The scallops extend over 22 stitches of the previous row, so it is better to make the corners first and to count the stitches both ways so as to distribute the stitches that are left over, between the scallops.

Corner scallop—Fasten the thread to the left of the second of the stitches that were added to make the turn, make 6 chain, 1 single on the 4th double crochet to the right = 1 single on the next double crochet = turn the work = * 2 chain, 1 double crochet on the 6th chain, repeat 7 times from *, in all 8 double crochets = after the 8th treble: 2 chain, skip 1 treble, 1 single on the 2 next double crochets = turn the work = 2 chain, 1 cluster stitch between each treble, in all 9 cluster stitches, then 2 chain, skip 2 double crochets, 1 single stitch on the next 2 double crochets = turn the work = 2 chain, 1 cluster stitch over the 1st, 2nd, 3rd, and 4th pairs of chain stitches in the preceding row, and 2 cluster stitches and 2 chain over the 5th, 6th and 7th chain stitches; over the other chain stitches again: 1 cluster stitch; then 2 chain, skip 2 double crochets, join to the 3rd double crochet = fasten off.

For the scallops on the right side, divide the stitches between the corner scallops into equal portions. Supposing that they are divisible by 22, count 9 stitches to the right, fasten the thread at the 9th; * 7 chain, skip 2 double crochets of the row beneath, 1 slip on the 3rd, 1 single stitch on the next = turn the work = 2 chain, 1 double crochet on the 7 chain, repeat 5 times from * and finish with 2 chain, 1 single on the 2nd lower treble, 1 single on the next double crochet = turn the work = 2 chain and 1 cluster stitch between each double crochet of the preceding row, 2 cluster stitches between the 3rd and 2nd double crochets = after the 8th stitch: 2 chain, skip 1 treble, 1 single on each of the 2 next stitches = repeat 3 times over 2 chain stitches of the previous row: 2 chain, 1 cluster stitch = on the 4th, 5th, and 6th chain stitches: 2 cluster and 2 chain; on the 3 last chain the same stitches as on the 3 first = then 1 single over each of the next 18 and repeat from *.

The final row consists of open picots formed of 5 chain stitches and 1 slip between each cluster stitch; after the last of these stitches and in the indent of the scallops on the straight line, only 2 chain stitches and 1 slip on the 3rd stitch.

Figure 478

Pattern in squares for counterpanes

(Fig. 478).—This pattern may be worked in the same stitch as the previous one, either in Tunisian crochet or in any other of the stitches already described.

Materials: Coton à tricoter DMC Nos. 6 to 12, Cordonnet 6 fils DMC Nos. 1 to 5, or Coton pour crochet DMC Nos. 6 to 12. Colors: Gris-Coutil 323 and Brun-Caroubier 303 or Bleu-cendré 448 and Rouge-Cornouille 449, Vert-Mousse 470 and Bleu d'Azur 3325.[A]

Make a foundation chain of 18 stitches on which you work 10 rows back and forth in the dark color. The 11th through the 21st rows are worked in the light color. After the 21st row, take up the dark color again. Each stripe should be 3 squares long.

The 2nd stripe is begun in the light color, and the stitches made at the beginning of each row are joined to those of the first stripe, as the stitches of the 3rd are to those of the 2nd and so on.

When you have made sufficiently large squares, each consisting of 9 small ones, border them with seven rows of slip stitches, worked back and forth. The 4 squares that form the corners are only to be bordered in this manner on two sides; the squares along the straight edges, on 3 sides, and only those that are intended for the center of the counterpane, on all 4 sides. The separate parts are then either sewn or crocheted together on the wrong side. The dark squares are ornamented with small stars worked in the light color, and the light squares with scallops in the dark color.

For the small stars—4 chain, close the ring; 2 slip on each stitch of the chain; 8 slip in all = after the 8th stitch: 8 chain, 1 slip on the 1st slip of the 8 slip stitches. Repeat the 8 chain 7 times and fasten off, then sew the star on in the center of the dark square, taking care to spread out the little points formed of chain stitches at regular distances from each other. The scallops are worked from left to right; fasten the thread on at the point where 4 squares touch, then make a chain of 18 stitches and secure it at the opposite point. On the chain stitches: 6 slip, 1 picot, 7 slip, 1 picot, 7 slip, 1 picot, 6 slip = fasten off.

Repeat the same scallop over the second half of the square; when you come to the 2nd picot of the first scallop, join the two picots. When both scallops are completed, fasten them on to the foundation by a few stitches on the wrong side.

The outside border of the counterpane is made separately and is worked inward from without, from left to right.

1st row—begin with the dark color and make * 10 chain stitches, drop the loop, put the needle into the 1st of the 10 chain, take up the loop and draw it through the stitch; 2 chain. On the 10 stitches: 6 double crochets quite close together. Repeat from * and go on repeating the sequence until the lace is long enough to trim the counterpane handsomely.

2nd row—in the light color and similar to the 1st = except that in joining the chain stitches together, you make the single stitch on the chain stitches of the 1st row.

3rd row—in the dark color and similar to the 2nd.

4th, 5th and 6th rows—in the light color and from right to left: 7 chain, 2 slip on each loop of chain stitches of the previous row.

7th row—in the light color and from left to right: * 2 slip on the double crochet of the lace, 11 chain, 2 slip on the next loop of chain stitches = these 2 stitches are made on the wrong side of the work = drop the loop, turn the work to the right, 3 slip on the last 3 chain, 8 chain **, and repeat, always from * to **.

One row of slip made on each chain stitch and a 2nd row of double crochets on the slip stitches completes the lace edging, which is afterward sewn onto the counterpane.

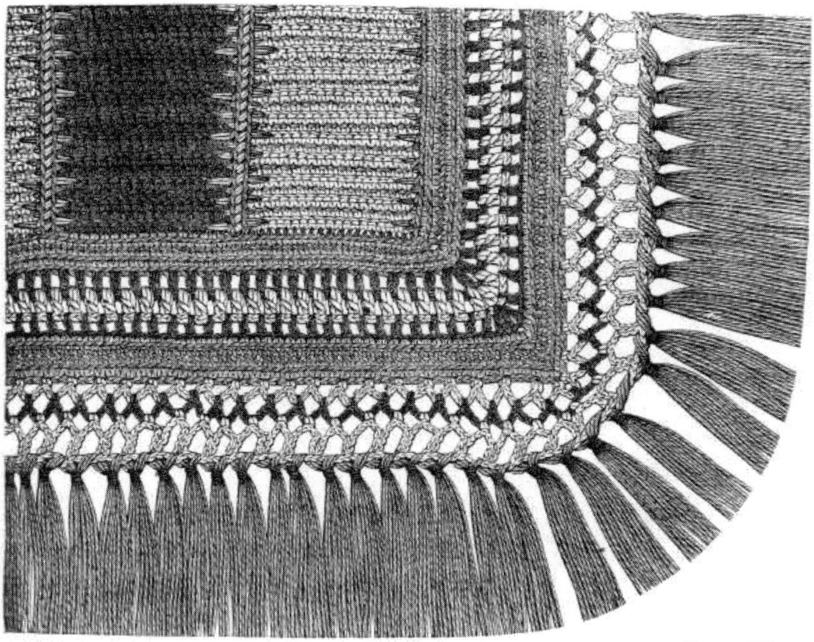

Figure 479

Counterpane with fringed border

(Fig. 479).—This pattern requires three colors; we suggest the following combination: Rouge-Turc 321, Bleu-Indigo 311 and white.

Materials: Coton pour crochet DMC Nos. 6 to 10, or Coton à tricoter DMC Nos. 6 to 14. Colors: White, Gris-Tilleul 331 and Rouge-Cornouille 449.[A]

The stripes—one red, the other blue—may be worked in any stitch. They are edged with 8 slip stitches of 3 different lengths, worked in red. * The first stitch passes only under the loops of the stitches; the 2nd over 2 stitches; the 3rd over 1; the 4th inward, over 3. Repeat from *.

These stitches must be worked parallel to each other along the two edges that are to be joined together.

The stripes are fastened together on the wrong side by single or slip stitches.

The outside edge consists of 15 rows: **1st row**—in red: 1 row of slip stitches on the right side of the work.

2nd row—in red, and on the wrong side of the work: slip stitches.

3rd and 4th rows—in red, and on the right side of the work: slip stitches.

5th row—in dark blue and on the right side: 1 treble, 1 chain, skip 1 slip of the row beneath, 1 treble, and so on.

6th row—in white, and similar to the 5th.

7th row—in blue, and similar to the 5th.

8th row—in red: 1 slip on each stitch of the preceding row.

9th row—in red and on the wrong side: 1 slip on each stitch of the preceding row.

10th and 11th rows—in red: both on the right side, 2 rows of slip stitches.

12th row—in white: 5 chain, skip 3, 1 slip on the 4th stitch.

13th row—in dark blue and similar to the 12th.

14th row—in white: * 1 slip on the 5th stitch of the blue row; 10 chain, drop the loop, lay the chain stitches from left to right, put the needle into the 3rd chain stitch, counting from the beginning, take up the loop and draw it through the 3rd chain stitch, 2 chain, and repeat from *.

15th row—in white: 1 slip on the picot formed by the chain stitches; 5 chain, 1 slip.

Into this last row, draw clusters of lengths of red cotton to form the fringe and knot them together with blue, or if you prefer it, you may finish off the coverlet with a hairpin fringe.

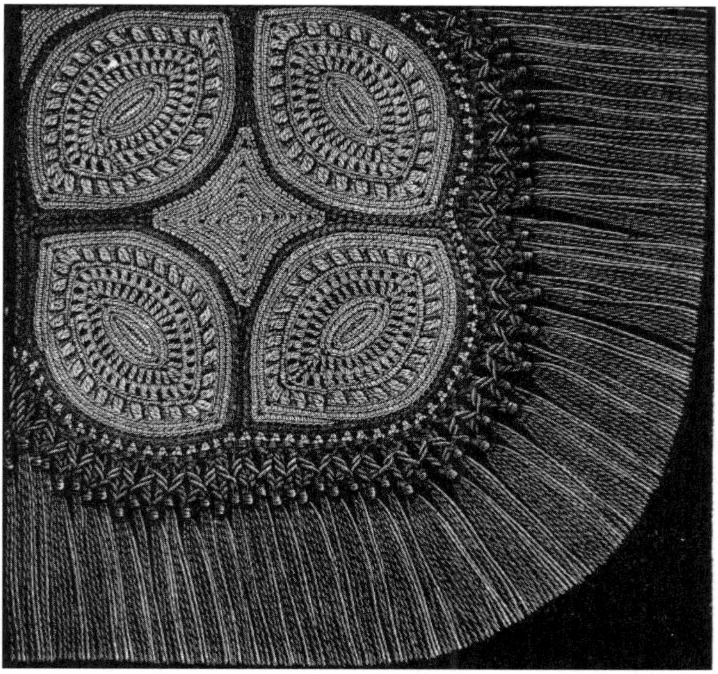

Figure 480

Counterpane composed of squares and olive-shaped figures

(Fig. 480).—There are many who shrink from undertaking a large piece of work because it becomes inconvenient to handle and carry about. The counterpane represented here has the advantage of being made up of a number of little pieces, which are worked separately and joined together afterward.

Materials: Coton pour crochet DMC Nos. 6 to 10, or Coton à tricoter DMC Nos. 6 to 10.

Colors: White and Rouge-Turc 321, or Écru and Rouge-Cerise 3318, Gris-Coutil 323 and Bleu-Gentiane 478.[A]

Two colors, which can be clearly distinguished from each other in the picture, should be chosen from among the various combinations suggested. One of them should be very light, say, cream or white, for the olive-shaped figures and squares, and the other of some soft shade only darker, for the connecting rows and the knotted fringe described in the chapter on Macramé.

The olive-shaped figures begin with 9 chain stitches, on which you make 8 slip stitches, and on the 9th, 3 slip for the corner.

On the second side of the chain: 8 slip and 3 besides on the corner stitch, and so on for 3 rows; in the last row, there should be 28 stitches.

These 3 rows are to be considered as one only.

2nd row—3 chain, 1 double crochet on the slip stitch that follows * 1 chain, 1 double crochet and repeat 11 times from *; 1 chain, 3 double crochets with 1 chain between them on the corner stitch, ** 1 chain, 1 treble, repeat 12 times from **.

On the last stitch at the corner, again 3 double crochets with 1 chain; close the round with 1 single stitch.

3rd row—1 chain, 1 single on the chain stitch that follows the 1st double crochet of the last row; 3 chain, 1 treble between the lower double crochets, 1 chain and so on, until you have 35 double crochets, counting the two sets of 3 double crochets at the corner.

4th row—here you can change the color: 1 slip on each of the stitches of the last row; 3 slip at the corners.

5th row—similar to the 4th.

6th row—2 slip, 1 cluster of 2 trebles on the same stitch of the 4th row as the 5th stitch of the last row is on; skip 1 slip.

Continue in this manner along the whole row, taking care that the 9th and 22nd cluster come just at the corner.

7th and 8th rows—these two last rows should be worked in the same color as the inside of the figure.

Be careful to make the increase at the point. A 9th row in the dark color may further be added to connect the figures by passing the thread from the wrong side to the right, between the 13 last stitches of two of the points of the figures. The space between these olive-shaped figures is filled by a pointed square of chain stitches.

In the 1st and following rows, skip 5 stitches at the point where the figures meet and continue to decrease in this manner until the space is filled up. The fringe is made in the dark color, either directly on to the slip crochet or after a few rows of open-work.

Figure 481

Squares for chair-backs

(Fig. 481).—This is a design for cut-work out of an old collection by Sibmacher, which we have adapted to crochet. It will be found most effective, worked in any of the given materials; we have worked it with admirable result, both in Cordonnet 6 fils DMC No. 15 and Fil à dentelle DMC No. 150.

Materials: Fil d'Alsace DMC Nos. 30 to 100, Cordonnet 6 fils DMC Nos. 20 to 50, or Fil à dentelle DMC Nos. 25 to 70 in white or écru.[A]

1st row—4 chain, close the ring.

2nd row—1 chain, 2 slip on each chain, 8 in all. Draw the loop of the last stitch through the 1st chain.

3rd row—6 chain, 1 double crochet *, 3 chain, 1 treble, repeat 6 times from *. In all, with the 3 chain, 8 double crochets.

4th row—4 slip, over each double crochet of 3 chain.

5th row—6 chain, 1 slip on the 2nd of the slip stitches beneath, * 3 chain, 1 treble, over the double crochet beneath, 3 chain, 1 slip on the 2nd stitch of the row beneath. Repeat 6 times from *, then add 3 chain, 1 slip on the 3rd of the 6 chain.

6th row—7 chain, 1 slip over the double crochet of the last row; repeat the same series 7 times.

7th row—3 chain, 1 double crochet over the double crochet beneath; 1 double crochet on each chain stitch, 2 double crochets on each slip stitch of the row beneath; in all, 72 double crochets, including the 3 chain.

8th row—* 8 chain, 1 slip between the 2 double crochets that were added between the 8th and the 9th = turn the work = make 12 slip on the wrong side = turn the work back to the right side = take up 1 loop of each of the 12 stitches for the Tunisian stitch that is made on 10 rows, and decrease by one stitch in each row, alternately on the right and left = draw up the 3 last loops together and make, descending on the right side 1 single stitch on each row of the pyramid you have just made, finish with 1 slip on the stitch that follows the 8 chain. Repeat 7 times from *.

9th row—all along the pyramid: 3 slip, 1 picot, 3 slip, 1 picot, 3 slip, 1 picot, 2 slip, 2 slip at the point. Repeat the same number of stitches on the 2nd side, and down the sides of all the pyramids = after the 9th row, fasten off.

10th row—fasten on the thread at a stitch at the point of a pyramid, * 7 chain, 5 overs, join the loop to the 2nd picot on the side of the pyramid where you are working, draw the needle back through 2 overs, make 2 overs more, and put the needle into the middle picot opposite and draw the needle twice through 2 loops, three times through 3, and each time after that, through 2 loops = 6 chain, 1 treble, join to the 3rd over, 7 chain, 1 slip = on the next pyramid 7 chain, 1 sextuple treble, join it to the next middle picot = draw the needle thrice through 2 loops, 1 double treble to join to the middle picot opposite, draw the needle back through the loops, and at the 4th over, through 3 loops, and each time after that, through 2 loops, 7 chain, 1 triple treble, join it to the 4th over, 7 chain, 1 double treble, 7 chain, 1 slip on the next pyramid. Repeat 3 times from *.

11th row—1 chain, 1 slip on each of the stitches of the previous row and 2 slip on those forming the corner; fasten off.

12th row—1 single on the first slip, 5 chain, 1 double crochet on the 3rd slip, 2 chain, 1 double crochet on the 3rd slip and so on to the corner and until you have 14 double crochets = on the corner stitch: 2 chain and 1 double crochet more; then proceed as you did on the first side. There should be 18 double crochets and 19 times 2 chains between the corner double crochets; all four sides should be alike.

13th row—1 slip on each stitch of the last row, not counting the 3 which are to be made at the corner.

14th row—14 single over the preceding stitches *, 1 chain, 24 slip; skip

4 slip of the last row, not counting the 2 increased stitches which must be left empty = after the 24th stitch, turn the work, skip 2, 21 slip, passing the needle under the 2 loops of the row beneath = turn the work = 1 chain, 20 slip = turn the work = 19 slip = continue to decrease in the same proportion until you have 3 stitches left and fasten off. In all the intakes, skip the next to last stitch coming back, and the 1st going, and always begin on the right side with 1 chain.

For the second half of the triangular figures which are worked from right to left, fasten on the thread to the 5th stitch after the increase and make 24 slip = 7 slip should remain between the two triangular figures formed of slip stitches = turn the work = 21 slip, skip the 2 last stitches, 1 slip on the stitch the thread is fastened to = turn the work = skip 1 stitch, 19 slip, 5 overs, put the needle through the 4th of the 7 stitches between, bring it back twice, each time through 2 loops, make 2 overs more, put the needle through the last stitch of the 3rd row opposite, bring it back twice through 2 loops, then once through 3 loops and twice through 2 loops = turn the work = 18 slip and so on, until you have made 10 transverse double crochets = fasten off; then repeat the same series of rows on the other sides.

15th row—do not cut off the thread on the 4th side but work backward: 3 single over the chain, 5 chain * 1 double crochet on the stitch from where the 5 chain proceeded, 2 chain, 1 double crochet on the last slip of the first half of the close parts of the pattern; 2 chain, 1 double crochet in the middle of the first part of the 10th transverse treble; 2 chain, 1 double crochet on the second half of the preceding treble, 2 chain, 1 double crochet on the 1st slip of the second half of the close parts; 2 chain, 1 double crochet on the 3rd and last upper stitch of the close part; 2 chain, 1 double crochet on the same stitch as the last treble. Then along the edge, 10 double crochets, joined by 2 chain, one of which double crochets should always be on a row of slip stitches = after the 10th treble: 3 chain, 1 slip on the 5th slip of the 13th row, 3 chain, again 11 double crochets connected by 2 chain = after the 11 double crochets: 2 chain ** and repeat 3 times from * to **.

16th row—on every 2 chain stitches: 3 slip.

17th row—7 chain, 1 slip on the 6th slip of the last row; repeat 7 times = for the 9th and 10th scallops only: * 5 chain. The slip stitch that follows the 9th scallop should come exactly over the corner stitch of the 13th row = after the 10th scallop: 1 slip; then 13 scallops with 7 chain, 1 slip on the 6th 5 stitch of the row beneath. Repeat twice from * = after the 4th scallop 2 smaller scallops, and up to the end of the row, 5 scallops more of 7 chain each.

18th row—make 7 slip over 7 chain, 5 chain, drop the treble, bring the needle back with the loop through the 3rd slip = on the 5 chain: 3 slip, 1 picot, 3 slip = on the 7 remaining stitches: 2 slip—on the 9th scallop of 5 chain, only: 5 slip = on the 10th scallop of 5 chain, only: 3 slip = then 7 chain, bring them back and join them to the 3rd slip of the 9th scallop and finish the picot.

When these squares are used in any number and have to be joined together, you must join 13 picots and leave the 14th free. The four empty picots in the center are connected by a small star.

Figure 482

Crochet star

(Fig. 482).—This is one of the most graceful and delicate crochet patterns we know. For the purpose of reproduction here, we have had it worked in all the different sizes of DMC cotton, but it looks best in a fine material; in Fil à dentelle No. 150, it can be compared to the finest needle-made lace.

Materials: Fil d'Alsace DMC No. 30, Cordonnet 6 fils DMC Nos. 25 to 80, or Fil à dentelle DMC Nos. 25 to 150.[A]

1st row—6 chain, close the ring.

2nd row—9 chain, 1 treble, * 4 chain, 1 treble; repeat 6 times from * = after the 7th treble: 4 chain, 1 single on the 5th of the 9 chain.

3rd row—1 chain, 4 slip, * 1 picot, 4 slip; repeat 7 times from * = carry the thread to the last stitch through the 1st slip.

4th row—12 chain, 1 double crochet on the stitch over the double crochet beneath, * 9 chain, 1 treble; repeat 6 times from * = after the 7th double crochet and the 9 chain: 1 single on the 3rd of the 12 chain.

5th row—3 chain, 1 double crochet on each stitch of the row beneath; including the 3 chain, 80 double crochets in the whole circumference =

after the last treble: 1 single on the 3 chain.

6th row—11 chain, 1 triple treble on the 2nd double crochet of the last row; 4 chain, 1 triple treble on the 3rd double crochet and so on, in all, 32 double crochets including the 7 chain.

7th row—1 chain, 5 slip on 4 chain.

8th row—3 slip on the 3 first chain, * 16 chain, skip 1, ** 1 single, 1 slip, 1 half double crochet, 2 double crochets, 1 double crochet 1½ long, 2 trebles, 1 double treble, 1 double crochet 3½ double crochets long, 1 quadruple-treble ***, 3 chain, skip 4 slip of the 7th row, 5 slip, 16 chain, join them, counting upward from below, to the 5th double crochet of the first pyramid = on 7 chain: 3 slip, 1 picot, 3 slip, 1 picot, 3 slip, 1 picot, 3 slip; join the last loop of the last slip and the loop of the 7th chain; 8 chain. Repeat from ** to *** = on the middle of the last triple treble: 1 treble toward the bottom, finish the treble, 3 chain, skip 4, 5 slip ****. Repeat 7 times from * to ****.

Coming back to the 1st point, make along it: 8 single stitches and then 7 chain, join them to the 5th double crochet of the 16th point = over the chain: 3 slip, 1 picot, 3 slip, 1 picot, 3 slip, 1 picot, 3 slip and finish with 9 single to carry the thread to the top of the point.

9th row—1 chain, 1 slip, * 15 chain, 1 slip at the top of the point and repeat 15 times from *.

10th row—3 chain; 1 double crochet on each stitch of the 9th row; 256 double crochets in all, including the 3 chain.

11th row—The star is bordered by small and large scallops, surmounted by points similar to those inside.

Begin by the small scallop, and on the 10th row, make 5 single, * 8 chain, bring them back and join them to the 1st of the 5 single; 1 slip, 8 chain, skip 4 double crochets, join them to the 5th; 14 slip on the 8 chain, 6 slip on the first 8 chain = turn the work = 5 chain, 1 double crochet on the slip stitch between two scallops; 5 chain, 1 slip on the 7th slip of the 1st scallop; 2 slip in the 5th chain, 2 chain, 1 picot, 10 chain, skip 1, and make on the following ones: 1 single, 1 slip, 1 half double crochet, 2 double crochets, 1 double crochet 1½ double crochet long, 1 picot, 2 chain, 2 slip on the 5 chain; 8 slip on the 8 chain.

To pass to the large scallop, make 16 single, 8 chain, bring them back, 1 slip on the 5th single, 8 chain, bring them back again to the 5th = turn the work = on the second set of 8 chain: 6 slip, 1 picot, 9 slip = on the first 8: 6 slip, then 8 chain, bring them back and join them to the 4th slip behind the picot of the finished scallop = on the 8 chain: 5 slip, 1 picot, 5 slip,

1 picot, 5 slip = on the remaining chain below, 3 slip, 1 picot, 6 slip; add 4 single on the double crochets and pass to the outer scallop = 18 chain, 1 slip on the 3rd of the 5 slip of the small upper scallop; 18 chain, 1 slip on the 4th of the 16 single = turn the work = 25 slip on the last chain stitches, and 25 on the first; 1 single on the 3rd single = turn the work = 1 slip on each of the preceding 50 slip stitches; join the last to the under row with a single stitch = turn the work = 10 slip, 1 picot, 3 slip, 1 picot, 3 slip, 1 picot, 4 slip, 2 chain, 1 picot, 10 chain, skip 1, 1 single, 1 slip, 1 half double crochet, 2 double crochets, 1 double crochet 1½ double crochet long, 1 treble, 1 double crochet 2½ double crochets long, 1 double treble, 1 picot, 2 chain and join them to the 6th slip stitch, counting from the middle.

Then 4 slip, 1 picot, 3 slip, 1 picot, 3 slip, 1 picot, 10 slip, 11 single on the double crochets. Repeat 7 times from *.

Figure 483

Star with little squares

(Fig. 483).—Begin with 4 chain stitches, close the ring.

Materials: The same as for fig. 482.

1st row—5 chain, * 1 treble, 2 chain. Repeat 6 times from *, to number altogether 8 double crochets including the 5 chain; 1 single on the 3rd chain.

2nd row—6 chain, * 1 double treble on the 1st chain stitch, 2 chain. Repeat 23 times from * and join to the 4th chain.

3rd row—6 chain, * 1 treble on the double crochet beneath, 3 chain. Repeat from * through the row; join to the 4th chain.

4th row—1 slip on the double crochet = on the 3 chain: 5 slip, 1 slip on the treble; work 5 times to and fro over these stitches, put the needle through the 2 threads of the last stitch = after the 5th row: 10 chain, then 5 slip on the 3 next chain.

In turning the work and going from the 2nd to the 3rd row, from the 4th to the 5th row, carry the thread behind the chain stitches so that they may blend with the slip stitches; make in all 12 little squares with 11 spaces between; after the 12th square: 5 chain, 1 single on the 5th row of the first square.

5th row—on each of the 6 slip of the 1st square: 1 single = on the 7th: 1 slip = 7 slip on the 5 chain = 1 slip on the 1st stitch of the 2nd square = 6 rows of slip, 14 chain, 1 slip on the 5th stitch of the next square = then make 6 rows of slip and wind the thread round the chain stitches.

6th row—1 single on every stitch of the last square, 1 slip on the last stitch above the 7 chain = on the 7 chain: 9 slip, 1 slip on the 1st stitch of the next square below = 9 rows to and fro.

7th row—after the 12th square: 9 chain, 1 single on the 1st slip, * 14 chain, 1 slip on the last slip = on the 9 chain: ** 1 chain, 1 slip, 1 double crochet 1½ double crochet long, 2 trebles 2½ double crochets long ***, 5 triple double crochets ****. Repeat from *** to **; then proceed from * to ****.

8th row—19 slip over the 14 chain, 1 single on each treble; stop them at the 12th square and at the 3rd double treble.

9th row—12 chain, 1 slip on the 10th of the 19 slip; 12 chain, 1 slip on the double treble, and proceed in the same way throughout the whole length of the row.

10th row—on the first 12 chain stitches: * 5 slip, 1 picot, 12 slip = on the second 12 chain: 7 slip, 10 chain, bring them back to the 5th of the 12 slip of the first scallop = on the 10 chain: 4 slip, 1 picot, 4 slip, 1 picot, 4 slip, 1 picot, 4 slip, = on the 12 chain: 5 slip, 1 picot, 7 slip. Repeat 12 times from *.

Figure 484

Crochet collar

(Fig. 484).—We have avoided as far as possible describing patterns in this book subject to the changes of fashion. This collar, composed of squares, stars, lozenge-shaped figures and a lace edge, is of a shape that will never be out of date. Fine and delicate work like this can only be executed in a very fine material, and we recommend unbleached thread over white. The soft tone and the gloss of unbleached thread give the work an antique look, unobtainable in a white material. Fil à dentelle DMC No. 120 is the best for the purpose.

Materials: Fil d'Alsace DMC No. 100, Cordonnet 6 fils DMC No. 120 or Fil à dentelle DMC No. 120, écru.

Begin with the straight-edged figures, and then make the connecting pieces between. The four squares with half stars at both ends of the collar and on the right and left of the center square have their four sides all alike, whereas the 3 figures within the scalloped edge are narrower on the outer than on the inner side where they join to the foundation.

Inner squares:

1st row—4 chain, close the ring; 5 chain, * 1 double crochet on the ring, 2 chain; repeat 6 times from * and fasten the thread to the 3rd chain stitch.

2nd row—1 chain, 3 slip over 2 chain; 1 slip over each treble.

3rd row—8 chain, * 1 double crochet on each double crochet of the 1st row, 6 chain. Repeat 6 times from * = 8 double crochets in all, including the first chain stitches.

4th row—* 10 chain; returning over the chain stitches: 1 slip, 1 half double crochet, 4 double crochets, 1 half double crochet, 1 slip, join to the 1st chain stitch = on the 6 chain of the 3rd row: ** 1 slip, 1 half double crochet, 1 treble, 3 trebles, 1 treble, 1 half double crochet, 1 slip ***. Repeat once more from ** to ***, then 3 times from * to *** = along the first leaf to the 10th stitch: 10 single.

5th row—starting from the point: * 7 chain, 1 double treble on the 5th stitch of the small scallop of the 4th row: 7 chain, 1 double treble on the next scallop, 7 chain, 1 slip on the 10th stitch of the 2nd leaf. Repeat 3 times from *.

6th row—1 chain, * 3 slip on the stitch that forms the point of the leaf; 1 slip on each chain stitch and each double crochet of the last row = 16 stitches in all, up to the 2nd double crochet = turn the work = coming back: 1 chain, 1 treble on the 4th slip, 1 chain, 1 treble, 1 chain, 1 treble, 1 chain, 1 treble, 1 chain, 1 treble, 1 chain, skip 3 slip, join to the 4th slip = turn the work = make on each chain stitch 2 slip and on each double crochet 1 slip and 1 picot over the 1st, 2nd, 4th and 5th treble; 8 slip **. Repeat 3 times from * to **.

7th row—1 chain, 1 slip on the 2nd of the 3 stitches at the point, * 9 chain, 1 treble between the two first picots of the semicircle formed in the last row; 8 chain, 1 double treble on the 3rd double crochet of the semicircle, 8 chain, 1 treble between the 3rd and 4th picots of the semicircle, 9 chain, 1 slip on the stitch at the corner.

8th row—19 single on the chain stitches of the 7th row, 1 chain, 3 slip on the corner stitch, 24 slip on the chain stitches and double crochets = turn the work = coming back: 2 chain, 1 treble on the 20th slip; on the same stitch add: 2 trebles with 2 chain; finish with: 2 chain, join them to the 5th slip = turn the work = on the chain stitches: 1 slip, 1 picot, 1 slip, 1 slip on the treble. Repeat this series 4 times = add: 4 slip on the chain stitches of the 7th row = turn the work = 5 chain, 1 treble on the 1st double crochet of the small semicircle; then again 3 times, 3 chain, and twice 1 treble on each of the double crochets beneath = after the last 5 chain: join to the 4th slip.

The points in this row are made with: * 1 slip on the chain stitches, 8 chain, skip 1 stitch = coming back: 1 single, 1 slip, 1 half double crochet, 1 double crochet 1½ double crochet long, 3 trebles, 1 slip on the 5 chain stitches. The 2nd point must be placed half before and the other half behind the picot; make altogether 7 points = after the 7th: 8 slip on the chain stitches of the 7th row = then work backward, without turning the work: 7 chain, 1 chain on the stitch at the top of the point and repeat 7 times from * = after the 8th set of 7 chain stitches: 1 chain; 1 slip on the 9th slip, bringing the thread forward from the right side to the wrong = 2 chain; take the thread back to the 3rd slip from the wrong side to the right = 1 double crochet on each chain stitch, 1 picot above each point, add 4 double crochets and 14 chain, join them to the 4th double crochet that comes after the 1st picot.

On the 14th chain: 5 slip, 1 picot, 4 slip, 1 picot, 4 slip, 1 picot, 5 slip, 4 double crochets to the next picot, 1 picot, 4 double crochets; 14 slip, join them to the double crochet nearest the 1st scallop and so on = make 7 scallops in all; after the 7th add 2 double crochets on the 2 chain stitches = after the 2nd double crochet make 2 slip, followed by the 3 stitches at the corner = in the next scallop, you fasten by 1 single, the 1st picot of the 1st scallop to the 3rd picot of the last scallop. When you have finished the four sides of the figure above-described, fasten off your thread.

Begin the edging of these squares on the narrower of the inner sides, and at the 3rd little scallop: * 1 slip on the middle picot of the 3rd little scallop, 7 chain, 1 treble on the 1st picot of the 4th scallop; 7 chain, 1 double treble on the 2nd picot of the same scallop, 6 chain, 1 treble on the 3rd picot of the same scallop, 6 chain, 1 slip on the middle picot of the 5th scallop; 10 chain, 1 double crochet on the middle picot of the 6th scallop, 11 chain **, 1 triple treble on the middle picot of the 7th and 1 triple treble on the middle picot of the 1st scallop following and draw the last loops of the 2 double crochets up together. Repeat once from * to **. Carry the double crochets all round the figure on the picots just referred to.

For the second half of the edging, which becomes a little wider: *** 10 chain, 1 double crochet on the 6th scallop, 11 chain, 2 triple trebles, the last loops of which you join to the middle picots of the 7th and 1st scallop; 11 chain, 1 double crochet in the next scallop; 10 chain, 1 double crochet in the 3rd scallop; 7 chain, 1 double crochet 2½ long, 8 chain, 1 double crochet 3½ long, 8 chain; 1 treble, 8 chain, 1 slip, 12 chain, 1 treble, 14 chain, **** 2 triple trebles, the last loops of which are joined together. Repeat from **** to ***, that is, the reverse way = finally add 1 more whole row of slip and 3 slip stitches at the corners = on the wider side, you should have 99 stitches, not counting the increases at the corner.

To make the same figure (forming a part of the large outside scallops), repeat the same rows you have in the inner square up to the 7th row, making the first half exactly the same as before. In the second half of the row of chains, there should be 1 chain stitch less in each intervening space than there was in the first half.

8th row—make the first half of this row like the 8th row of the inner square = over the 2nd half, one quarter of which is 4 chain stitches narrower, the little wheels are made like the others with 7 picots. The number of chain stitches and the double crochets of the setting are also the same, but instead of 7 points you have to make 5 and over these, 5 small scallops instead of 7.

The setting toward the top is made exactly in the same manner as the wide part of the upper square—that is, as from the 3rd scallop of the first semicircle to the 5th scallop of the 2nd. From this point, the series of stitches changes, so as to form a rounded edge: * 7 chain, 1 slip on the 6th scallop; 15 chain, 2 double trebles joined by the last loops to the 7th and 1st scallop; 14 chain, 1 slip on the 2nd of the 5 scallops; 15 chain, 1 slip on the 3rd scallop; 15 chain, 1 slip on the 4th scallop, 15 chain **, 2 double trebles joined by the last loops in the 5th and 1st scallop. Repeat once again from ** to * = add 1 row of slip on each stitch of the preceding row; 3 slip on the two top corner stitches. You will thus have 3 figures with a rounded edge on one side.

The second kind of square consists of 8 leaves inside and is begun in the same way by 6 chains formed into a ring.

1st row—5 chain, 1 treble, 2 chain, * 1 treble, 2 chain. Repeat 6 times from * and join to the 3rd of the 5 chain.

2nd row—1 chain, 3 slip over 2 chain, 1 slip on each treble.

3rd row—9 chain, * skip 1 stitch = coming back: 1 single, 1 slip, 1 half double crochet, 1 treble, 1 treble, 1 double treble, 1 double crochet over the double crochet of the 2nd row; 7 chain. Repeat 7 times from * = after the 8th point: 7 single along the 1st.

4th row—* 1 slip on the stitch you skipped at the point, 5 chain, 1 double treble on the double crochet of the 3rd row, 5 chain. Repeat 7 times from *.

5th row—3 chain, 1 double crochet on each stitch of the 4th row; join to the 3rd of the 3 chain.

6th row—10 chain, 1 slip on the double crochet over the double treble of the 4th row: 10 chain, 1 slip on the double crochet above the little point.

7th row—15 slip on the 10 chain = on the 3rd scallop only: * 7 slip, 10 chain, come back to the second scallop, bring the thread back from the wrong side to the right between the 7th and 8th slip stitches, 15 slip on the 3rd scallop, 8 slip on the next scallop, 15 slip and repeat 6 times from *.

When the 16th scallop is finished, pass to the point of the 1st scallop by means of 7 single, then add the 10 chain to pass to the 8th scallop above; when that is finished, fasten off, and fasten on again to one of the 8 scallops.

8th row—* 21 chain, skip 1 stitch, 1 slip, 1 half double crochet, 1 treble, 1 double crochet 1½ double crochet long, 1 treble, 1 double crochet 2½ double crochets long, 1 double treble, 1 double crochet 3½ double crochets long, 1 triple treble, 1 double crochet 4½ double crochets long, 1 quadruple treble. After passing through the 3rd loop, make 1 triple treble, between the 2 slip scallops; then finish the quadruple treble, 7 chain, 1 slip on the 2nd scallop and repeat 7 times from *.

9th row—* 7 slip on the 7 chain; 1 slip on each stitch of the pyramid, 3 slip on the stitch at the point; 4 slip on the 7 chain on the opposite side = turn the work = ** 1 chain, skip 1 slip, 1 double crochet on the 2nd stitch = after the 5th treble, leave out no more stitches between the double crochets ***; place the 8th, 9th and 10th double crochets on the 2nd of the increased stitches. Repeat on the opposite side from *** to ** and join to the 4th of the slip stitches = make 17 double crochets in all; then one slip over each chain, 1 slip on each double crochet and 1 picot after every 3rd slip = after the 4th and up to the 8th picot, leave only 2 slip between: 11 picots in all = in conclusion: 3 slip more on the 7 chain and repeat the whole 7 times from *.

Begin the little wheel at the top of the square with 10 chain for the ring = 16 slip on the ring, 4 chain, * 1 treble, 1 chain = repeat 14 times from *; 16 double crochets in all, including the chain stitches = then on each double crochet and each chain stitch: 1 slip; after 4 slip: 1 picot; connect the wheel first on the right.

The 2nd picot is to be fastened to the 9th picot of the large scallop = proceed with 3 times 4 slip with 1 picot = after the 3rd slip, fasten the picot to the 3rd picot of the next large scallop and complete the small wheel. The left wheel is made and inserted in the same manner as the right one. For the foundation ring of the wheels at the bottom of the square, require 14 chain, on which you make 21 slip = on these: 4 chain, * 1 treble, 1 chain = repeat 19 times from *; 21 double crochets in all, including the chain stitches = 3 slip, 1 picot, 3 slip, 1 picot, 3 slip, 1 picot, 3 slip, 4 chain, join to the 8th picot of the 2nd scallop; 4 chain, finish the picot, 3 slip, 1 picot, 3 slip, 8 chain, join to the 10th picot of the scallop, 8 chain, complete the picot; 3 slip, 1 picot, 3 slip, 8 chain, join to the 2nd picot of the 3rd scallop, 8 chain, close the picot, 3 chain, 1 picot, 3 slip, 4 chain, join to the 4th picot of the 3rd scallop; 4 chain, complete the picot, 3 slip, 1 picot and so on, until you have 14 picots round the wheel. Repeat the same wheel to the left between the 4th and 5th scallop.

The edging of this second kind of square is also slightly different. Fasten the thread to the 6th picot of the 1st scallop before the small wheel; then working from right to left, count:

* 10 chain, 1 double crochet on the 2nd empty picot of the small wheel; 8 chain, 1 double treble on the 4th picot of the wheel = upward: 9 chain, 1 treble on the 6th picot of the wheel; 9 chain, 1 slip on the 6th picot of the 8th scallop, 12 chain, 1 slip on the 7th picot of the scallop, 11 chain **, 1 triple treble on the 9th picot of the 8th scallop and on the 3rd picot of the 7th; draw the last loops of the two double crochets up together. Repeat once more from ** to *, then: 1 slip on the 6th picot of the 6th scallop; *** 12 chain, 1 quintuple treble on the 9th picot of the 6th scallop, retain 2 loops of the double crochet on the needle, make 4 more overs, join the double crochet to the 3rd picot of the 5th scallop; finish the bars, 12 chain, 1 slip in the 6th picot of the next scallop = 12 chain, 1 treble on the 2nd picot of the 7 empty picots of the bottom wheel; 9 chain, 1 triple treble on the 4th picot; 12 chain, 1 treble on the 6th picot, 14 chain, 1 slip on the 6th picot of the 4th scallop, 14 chain ***, 1 sextuple treble, in the 9th and 3rd picots of the 4th and 3rd scallops ****. For the preceding treble, you pass first through 4 loops only; then make 4 more overs for the other half of the treble, and finish the last loops one by one. Repeat from **** to ***. One row of slip stitches completes the square.

After you make the square similar to that of the upper one, you just have to add the large wheels at the top.

Begin the setting of chain stitches and double crochets at the first scallop between 2 wheels = 1 slip on the 6th picot of the 1st scallop; 14 chain, 2 quadruple trebles, of which the last loops only are joined together, on the 9th and 3rd picot of the 1st and 2nd scallop, = 14 chain, 1 slip on the 6th picot of the next scallop; * 14 chain, 1 double crochet on the 2nd empty picot of the wheel; 10 chain, 1 triple treble on the 4th picot, 10 chain, 1 double crochet on the 6th picot; 14 chain, 1 slip on the 6th picot of the 3rd scallop; 14 chain, 2 quintuple trebles on the 10th and 2nd picot of the 3rd and 4th scallop; 15 chain, 1 slip on the 6th picot of the 4th scallop; 16 chain, 2 quintuple trebles on the 10th and 2nd picot of the 4th and 5th scallop; 16 chain, 1 slip on the 6th picot of the 5th scallop; 15 chain ** 3 sextuple trebles on the 10th and 2nd picot of the 5th and 6th scallop. Repeat from ** to *; and make 4 figures with rounded edges. When all the figures are finished, join them together by double crochets of a suitable length.

Introduce the thread at the corner stitch on the widest side of the 2nd 8 pointed star and make: 1 slip, 6 chain, skip 3 stitches, 1 slip on the 3 next stitches, 4 chain, skip 2, 1 slip on the next 3 slip stitches.

Make 11 loops in this manner, each consisting of 4 chain and 3 slip; then 2 loops of 3 chain and 2 slip = then skip as many stitches of the square at the edge of the collar as were left empty in the second square; 2 slip and draw the loop each time through the 2 last stitches of the opposite square

= 1 chain, 1 single on the 2nd chain stitch of the opposite side; 1 chain, 3 slip on the edge of the first square, 1 chain, 1 single, 1 chain, skip 3 stitches, 3 slip, 5 chain, bring the loop from the wrong side to the right = on the chain stitches: 4 slip, 2 chain, skip 3, 3 slip.

From this point onward, fasten all the bars of chain stitches to the loops produced by the same stitches in the 2nd square. Thus, the 1st bar consists of 5 chain, the 2nd will consist of 7 chain on which make 7 slip, and then add 2 more chain. Nowhere must the two first chain stitches be uncovered.

The 3rd bar must consist of 9 chain, 9 slip and 2 chain = the 4th of 11 chain, 5 slip, 1 picot, 5 slip, 2 chain = the 5th of 13 chain, 4 slip, 1 picot, 4 slip, 1 picot, 4 slip, 2 chain = the 6th of 16 chain, 6 slip, 1 picot, 6 slip, 1 picot, 6 slip, 2 chain = the 7th of 18 chain, 5 slip, 1 picot, 4 slip, 1 picot, 4 slip, 1 picot, 5 slip, 2 chain = the 8th of 21 chain, 5 slip, 1 picot, 5 slip, 1 picot, 5 slip, 1 picot, 5 slip, 2 chain = the 9th of 24 chain, 5 slip, 1 picot, 5 slip, 1 picot, 5 slip, 1 picot, 5 slip, 1 picot, 5 slip, 2 chain = the 10th of 26 chain, 6 slip, 1 picot, 5 slip, 1 picot, 5 slip, 1 picot, 5 slip, 1 picot, 6 slip, 2 chain = the 11th and last of 28 chain, 32 slip, 2 chain, fasten off.

As the square with the semicircles in it has more slip stitches in the edge than the one with the eight-pointed star in it, the stitches must be divided so that you skip 3 from time to time instead of 2. When the 7 top figures are finished, join the 7 bottom ones to them, each separately, by a row of slip stitches, made on the wrong side of the work. Below the first square with the semicircles comes the eight-pointed star; below the next eight-pointed star, the square with the semicircles, and so on.

A narrow edging forms the outside border, the foundation of which is a row of slip stitches running all along the squares. At the middle of the square, you decrease by 2 stitches, and at the point where two squares meet, by 3. When you reach the left side and the end of the row, make 3 slip on the corner stitch, then: * 5 slip, 1 picot, 5 slip, 14 chain, join them to the first of the 5 first slip (drop the thread at each scallop and bring it forward from the wrong side to the right) = on the 14 chain: 5 slip, 1 picot, 11 slip, 1 picot, 5 slip = along the square: 5 slip, 1 picot, 5 slip, then 14 chain, join them to the first slip = over the 14 chain: 5 slip, 1 picot, 5 slip, 14 chain, join them in turning back between the 5th and 6th of the 10 slip of the 1st scallop; 5 slip, 1 picot, 5 slip, 1 picot, 5 slip, 1 picot, 5 slip; on the half-finished scallop: 5 slip, 1 picot, 5 slip ** = on the slip stitches of the edge: 4 slip, 1 picot, 4 slip, 12 chain, come back, join to the 1st of the 4 slip = on the 12 chain: 4 slip, 1 picot, 4 slip, 1 picot, 4 slip, 1 picot, 4 slip *** = repeat on the same figure once from * to *** and once from * to **.

This makes 77 stitches, the number needed on the wide side of the straight-edged figures.

The scallops vary a little on the rounded sides. There, you should have 110 stitches, counting from the corner to the double crochet that marks the middle at the bottom. The single scallops, between the triple scallops of the border, are also all made over 8 stitches; the first triple scallop is made over 20 stitches, the 2nd, 3rd and 4th triple scallop over 16 stitches.

Make no single scallop after the 4th triple one, which is immediately succeeded by the 5th triple scallop, over 16 stitches.

Around each star, there are 9 triple and 8 single scallops. After the 8th single one, make 3 slip stitches on the 2 chain stitches of the connecting bar.

On the 32 slip stitches of the last bar: 8 slip, 1 picot, 4 slip, 12 chain, bring them back and join to the 5th of the 8 slip = on the 12 chain: 5 slip, 2 chain, draw the loop through the picot in the middle of the last single scallop, 2 chain, close the picot, 8 slip, 1 picot, 5 slip = in the bar: 4 slip, 1 picot, 4 slip, 12 chain, bring them back and fasten them to the 1st slip = 5 slip, 1 picot, 4 slip, 12 chain, join them to the 4th slip of the 1st scallop; 5 slip, 1 picot, 8 slip, 1 picot, 5 slip = in the half-finished scallop: 4 slip, 1 picot, 4 slip = in the bar: 4 slip, 1 picot, 4 slip = 12 chain, bring them back and fasten them to the 1st slip. 4 slip, 1 picot, 4 slip, 12 chain, join them close to the scallop above = 5 slip, 1 picot, 4 slip, 12 chain, bring them back and join them to the 4th slip of the 2nd scallop; 5 slip, 1 picot, 5 slip, 1 picot, 5 slip, 1 picot, 5 slip = in each of the 2 half-finished scallops: 4 slip, 1 picot, 5 slip = finish with 4 slip, 3 slip on the 2 chain and repeat from * round all the rounded parts.

The lozenges that fill the empty spaces between the large figures are made in 7 rows, on a ring formed of 4 chain.

1st row—5 chain, 1 double crochet on the ring, 2 chain, 8 double crochets in all, including the bar of chain stitches.

2nd row—3 slip over 2 chain, 1 slip over each treble.

3rd row—7 chain, 1 double crochet over the double crochet beneath, 5 chain, 1 treble; 8 double crochets in all.

4th row—* 1 slip, 1 half double crochet, 1 treble, 1 treble, 1 double crochet 2½ double crochets long; ** repeat the reverse way to * = 1 slip on the treble, 7 chain, skip 1 stitch, 1 slip, 1 treble, 1 treble, 1 treble, 1 slip. Repeat twice from * to **, followed by: 9 chain, skip 1, 1 single, 1 slip, 1 half double crochet, 2 double crochets, 1 half double crochet, 1 slip, 1 single ***. Repeat once from * to ***, then again from * to **, and add 5 single all along the scallop.

5th row—9 chain * 1 slip on the top stitch of the small leaf, 7 chain, 1 double crochet on the middle stitch of the scallop, 7 chain, 1 double crochet on the next scallop = 9 chain, 1 slip on the leaf, 9 chain, 1 double crochet on the scallop, 7 chain, 1 double crochet on the next scallop, 7 chain and repeat once from *.

6th row—1 slip on each stitch of the row before, 3 slip on the points.

7th row—on each side of the lozenge 3 little scallops on 8 chain, with 3 picots and 1 picot below the scallops and between every 4 slip; the scallops at the points extend over 4 stitches only, so that the picot below is left out.

These lozenges are fastened on two sides to the middle picot of the triple scallop; then, starting from the 3rd scallop of the lozenge you make, 8 chain, join them to the middle picot of the 1st triple scallop; coming back over the 8 chain: 5 slip, 1 picot, 5 slip and finish the scallop. The next scallop, at the point of the lozenge, is fastened by a picot of 6 chain to the middle picot of the 6th scallop underneath the connecting bar. Repeat the same on the 2nd side and make 6 lozenges in all.

The lace that finishes off the collar at the neck must be made to stand up, and is begun by a row of double crochets on the slip stitches.

From the corner as far as the 2nd double crochet of the 4th scallop, make double trebles. From the 4th scallop to the 6th chain stitch after the 5th scallop, make trebles, from this point to the 2nd scallop of the next semicircle, only double crochets, then again trebles and finish with double trebles as at the beginning. Decrease by 2 or 3 stitches in each square.

When this row of double crochets is finished, fasten off, and fasten on again on the right and on the base of the 1st double crochet which you border with 4 chain. Then follow: * 15 slip on the row of double crochets, put the needle in under the 2 loops of the double crochets = turn the work = 2 chain, 1 treble, skip 4 slip, 1 treble on the 5th stitch, 2 chain, 1 treble, 2 chain, 1 treble, 2 chain, skip 4 slip = turn the work = bring the loop to the front; ** 1 slip, 1 picot, 1 slip, 1 slip on the treble; repeat 3 times again from ** and add 4 slip on the double crochets = turn the work = 6 chain, 1 treble over the double crochet beneath; again 3 times 6 chain stitches and 1 treble; join the 4th set of 6 chain to the 4th slip = bring the thread back to the front: 1 slip on the 6 chain = 8 chain, skip 1, and make on the others: 1 slip, 1 half double crochet, 2 double crochets, 1 double crochet 1½ double crochet long, 2 trebles, 1 slip stitch on the 6 chain. The next point comes above a treble; you make 7 points in all. After the 7th: 5 slip, then 7 chain, 1 slip on each point between the points and join.

Join the 8th set of 7 chain on to the 4th slip of the first double crochet = then add: 2 chain, draw the loop from the wrong side to the right through the 1st slip stitch; 8 double crochets,

1 picot, 4 double crochets, 12 chain, bring them back over the picot, join it between the 4th and 5th double crochets; 5 slip, 1 picot, 5 slip, 1 picot, 5 slip, 1 picot, 5 slip.

Over each point: 1 picot and over the picot 1 scallop, like the one made in the square. On the 7th point, only 1 picot = after the last double crochet on the last chain, 2 chain; then go on with the slip stitches until you have 27 and repeat from *.

In the semicircles that follow, you leave out the first and last little scallops, the first and the last scallop must be joined together by the first and the last picot; in the last semicircle, make 6 little scallops, the same as you did in the first.

Figure 485

Crochet chair-back

(Fig. 485).—The close leaves in slip stitch of the large center star and the 4 corner figures forming a cross and the diagonal figures all have to be made separately and sewn on afterward in their proper place. To join the separate parts neatly together, draw a square the size of the work on a piece of thick paper or waxcloth, divide it into 8 parts by means of straight and diagonal lines, sew the separate pieces of crochet upon it, faced downward in their proper places, and make the double crochets on the wrong side of the work.

Materials: Fil à dentelle DMC No. 50 for the close figures and No. 120 for the connecting bars.[A]

Begin by the center star and make: 12 chain, close the ring.

1st row—23 slip on the 12 chain.

2nd row—9 chain, 1 treble on the 2nd slip, 4 chain, 1 double crochet and so on until you have 12 double crochets, including the 5 chain.

3rd row—1 slip on each chain stitch and each treble; 60 slip in all.

4th row—3 slip, 1 picot, altogether 20 picots in the row, then fasten off.

The leaves round the ring have 3 petals, 1 large and 2 small; you begin by the large one and make the small ones afterward. Begin the petals from the point and not from the bottom as is generally done—30 chain; coming back: 4 single, 4 slip, 5 half double crochets, 8 double crochets, 4 half double crochets, 4 slip stitches, 3 slip on the 1st chain = on the second side of the chain make the same number of stitches but in the reverse order.

Small petal on the left—21 chain, skip 1, 5 slip, 3 half double crochets, 5 double crochets, 3 half double crochets, 3 slip, 3 slip on the top. Repeat the same series of stitches in the reverse order on the second side = at the 10th stitch of the large petal and counting upward from below, draw the thread through the 10th stitch of the small petal, and do the same through the 9 next stitches = for this purpose drop the loop each time and draw it back through the opposite stitch, from the wrong side to the right. After making the same petal on the right, fasten off; fasten on again at the outer edge and edge the 3 petals with 1 slip on each stitch and 3 slip on the stitch at the point; make 4 leaves with 3 petals each.

Between the pointed leaves, which are afterward placed on the diagonal line of the square, come some very long leaves which are rounded toward the top—29 chain, skip 1, 5 slip, 2 chain, 1 double crochet on the 3rd of the chain stitches; carry on the double crochets until you have, on coming to the last chain, 7 double crochets = turn the work and make 1 slip on each stitch of the row = turn the work = 1 slip on every stitch all round = turn the work = * 9 slip, 4 half double crochets, 3 double crochets, 2 trebles, join the last loops of the 2 last double crochets together; set the 20th and 21st treble on the same stitch = the 20th double crochet 2½ double crochets long; the 21st a double treble = on the next slip stitch; 1 double crochet 3½ double crochets long and 1 triple treble = again on the next stitch: 2 double crochets, the first of them 4½ double crochets long, the 2nd a quintuple one = on the 3rd slip: 2 quadruple trebles, 4 chain, 1 slip on the slip stitch of the 2nd row and next to the last quadruple treble, 1 half double crochet, 1 treble, 2 trebles on one stitch, 2 double trebles on one stitch **, 1 triple treble on the 2 next stitches. Repeat from ** to *, therefore in the reverse order.

To make the large star which is the first of the figures placed on the diagonal line, make: 4 chain, close the ring.

1st row—10 chain,* 1 treble on the 4 chain, 5 chain. Repeat 4 times from *, 6 double crochets in all.

2nd row—over 5 chain: 1 half double crochet, 1 treble, 1 double crochet 1½ double crochet long, 1 treble, 1 double crochet 2½ double crochets long **, 1 double treble. Repeat once from ** to * and 5 times from * to **.

3rd row—1 slip on each stitch of the 2nd row.

4th row—3 slip, 1 picot, 2 slip, * 2 chain, 1 picot, 5 chain, skip 1 = coming back: 4 slip, 1 picot, 2 slip = on the slip stitches of the 3rd row: 2 slip, 1 picot, 3 slip. Repeat from *, but this time make sure the double crochets that are placed over the half double crochets of the 2nd row are begin with 3 chain. Make, altogether, 12 long bars, 6 of them beginning with 2 chain and 6 with 3; these bars remain empty; after the 12th you fasten off.

5th row—fasten on the thread to the top stitch of a treble, 11 chain, 1 slip. Repeat this series 11 times.

6th and 7th rows—1 slip on each stitch of the 5th row, then 1 slip on each stitch of the 6th row.

8th row—over 9 bars and 8 spaces: 3 slip, 1 picot, 3 slip and so on. Add nothing further to the 2 rows of slip stitches of the 10th, 11th and 12th picots.

For the second star of the corner figure 4 chain, close.

1st row—8 chain, 1 treble, * 5 chain, 1 treble. Repeat 3 times from *; 5 double crochets in all, including the chain stitches.

2nd row—* 1 chain, 1 half double crochet, 1 treble, 1 double crochet 1½ double crochet long, 1 treble, 1 double treble **. Repeat from ** to *, and the whole series 4 times.

3rd row—* 1 chain, 3 slip, 1 picot, 2 slip, 2 chain, 1 picot, 4 chain = coming back, 4 slip on the 4 chain, 1 picot, 2 chain = on the stitches of the 2nd row: 2 slip, 1 picot, 2 slip, 3 chain, 1 picot, 5 chain, skip 1, 4 slip = coming back: 1 picot, 3 slip. Repeat 4 times from *, fasten off.

4th row—fasten on at the point of one of the bars and make from one bar to the other: 9 chain, 1 slip on each bar.

5th row—1 slip on each stitch of the last row.

6th row—1 slip on each stitch of the last row and join the 4 last stitches to the 4 that are under the 11th double crochet of the 1st star, taking care to put the double crochets one above the other.

The 3rd star also begins with 4 chain formed into a ring.

1st row—8 chain, 1 treble, 5 chain, 1 treble, 5 chain, 1 treble, 5 chain, join them to the 4th of the 8 chain.

2nd row—2 chain, * 1 half double crochet, 1 treble, 1 treble, 1½ double crochet long, 1 treble **. Repeat from ** to *, and then, 3 times from * to **.

3rd row—1 slip on each stitch of the 2nd row.

4th row—1 chain, 2 slip, * 1 picot, 3 chain, 1 picot, 5 chain. Repeat 3 times from *; after the 8th picot: 3 chain.

5th row—15 chain, 1 double treble on the 5th and on the 2nd slip stitch between 2 picots, 9 chain, 1 double treble and so on. Altogether, including the chain stitches, 8 double crochets and 8 times 9 chain; join to the 7th chain.

6th and 7th rows—1 slip on each stitch of the previous row; join the 4 last stitches again to the 4th stitch of the 2nd star and fasten off.

The open work border is made from the 1st large star, beginning near the 9th double crochet at the point where the picots leave off. After fastening on the thread, 5 chain, skip 2 slip, 1 slip on the 3rd = at the point where the circles meet, skip 3 or 4 stitches on each side and carry the double crochet over the indent of the scallop.

After finishing the picots of chain stitches on the two sides and as far as the 3rd double crochet of the large star, fasten off. Fasten on again on the right of the large star: 4 chain, 1 slip on the 3rd chain; put the needle only through the 2 upper loops of the chain stitch; in the indent, connect 3 picots by 1 chain stitch; 2 chain and 1 slip between the next slip stitches. Fasten off. The 2 next rows both begin on the right and consist of slip stitches only; in the indent of the rings join 3 stitches of the preceding row together by 1 slip.

The 5 leaves over the circles—Begin with the middle and largest one—25 chain, skip 1, 3 slip, 2 chain, skip 2, 1 treble, 2 chain and so on, 7 double crochets in all = turn the work = 1 slip on each stitch, passing under only 1 loop of the stitches = on the stitch you skipped: 3 slip; on the second side: 1 slip on each stitch = turn the work = do as in the last row = turn the work = do as in the 2 last rows, but leave the 5 last stitches untouched = turn the work = 15 slip, * 1 chain = turn the work = 12 slip = turn the work = 12 slip on the 12 slip and on all those you skipped **. Fasten off the thread. On the 2nd side of the leaf: draw the thread through the 6th stitch, counting upward from below and on the side that is not indented, 15 slip and repeat from * to ** = then make: 1 row of slip, putting the needle through both the loops of the lower stitches = at the points of the leaves: 3 slip, in the indents of the leaves skip 1 stitch.

First leaf on the right of the large leaf—25 chain, skip 1, 3 slip, 1 chain, 1 double crochet on the 3rd chain; 7 double crochets in all = turn the work = 1 slip on each stitch, 18 stitches altogether, to the corner stitch; 3 slip on the corner stitch. Work the 2nd side like the 1st.

Add 3 more rows of slip stitches and increase 3 slip on the stitch at the point = in the 3rd row leave the 5 last stitches empty = turn the work = 11 slip, 1 chain = turn the work = 11 slip and 5 slip on the 5 stitches that were passed over; fasten off.

On the opposite side, fasten the thread on the wrong side at the 8th stitch counting from the point: 12 slip, 1 chain = turn the work = 12 slip

= turn the work = make slip stitches up to the end of the leaf and border it, like the large leaf, with slip stitches = join the 8 first stitches to the corresponding ones in the large leaf = make 4 leaves all alike.

2nd leaf on the left—19 chain, skip 1, 3 slip, 2 chain, 1 double crochet on the 2nd chain; 7 double crochets in all = turn the work = 1 slip on each of the preceding stitches, 3 slip on the stitch at the point = turn the work = 1 row of slip stitches = turn the work = 1 row of slip = turn the work = 1 row of slip, excepting on the last 7 stitches = turn the work = 14 slip, 1 chain = 3 more rows to and fro with 11 slip; fasten off, and fasten on again on the 2nd side at the 6th stitch counting from below: 2 rows of 11 slip and 1 row to the end of the leaf = then encircle this leaf, like the others with slip stitches, join the 8 last stitches to the last 8 of the large leaf = make 4 leaves all alike.

3rd leaf on the right—18 chain, skip 1, 2 slip, 1 chain, 1 double crochet on the 3rd chain, 5 double crochets in all = turn the work = 4 rows of slip worked to and fro; on the stitch at the point: 3 slip = after the 4th row: 4 double crochets, 8 slip, 1 chain, 4 slip, 1 chain, 4 slip, 1 chain, then slip stitches to the end = fasten off. On the second side, fasten on to the 6th stitch counting downward from the top: 9 slip = coming back: 3 slip, 1 chain, 7 slip = coming back: 7 slip, 1 chain = then to the end of the leaf, 1 slip on each stitch.

3rd leaf on the left—14 chain, skip 1, 2 slip, 2 chain, 1 treble, 2 chain, 1 treble, 2 chain, 1 treble, 2 chain, 1 treble; 4 rows of slip all round, 3 slip on the stitch at the point, and 3 slip on the added stitch. After the 4th row: 14 slip = turn the work = 10 slip = turn the work = 3 single, 7 slip = coming back: 7 slip = coming back again: 7 slip; after the last slip, 1 single on each slip up to the top = fasten off.

On the second side of the leaf: 9 slip = turn the work = 5 slip = turn the work = 5 slip, 1 single on each of the remaining stitches = turn the work = surround the whole leaf with slip stitches; 3 slip on each stitch at the point; join the 8 last stitches to the 8 last of the 2nd leaf.

Branch on the right and 1st leaf—28 chain, skip 1, 4 slip, 1 chain, 1 double crochet on the 3rd chain, 1 chain, 1 double crochet on the 3rd chain, 1 chain, 1 double crochet 1½ double crochet long on the 3rd chain, 1 chain, 1 double crochet 1½ double crochet long on the 3rd chain, 1 chain, 1 double crochet on the 3rd chain, 1 chain, 1 half double crochet on the 3rd chain, 1 chain, skip 2 stitches, 5 slip = on the second side of the chain: * 1 slip on each stitch, 3 slip on the 2nd of the skipped stitches. Repeat 3 times from *. After the 4th row of slip: 6 chain = turn the work = 1 row of slip on both sides and slip stitches on the 6 chain; fasten off the thread. Counting back the last stitches, fasten on the thread at the 18th stitch, make one more row of slip, fasten off.

2nd leaf of the branch—22 chain, skip 1, 3 slip, 1 chain, 1 half double crochet on the 3rd chain, 1 chain, 1 double crochet on the 3rd chain, 1 chain, 1 double crochet on the 3rd chain, 1 chain, 1 half double crochet on the 3rd chain, 1 chain, 1 slip on the 3rd chain, 1 slip on each of the remaining stitches; 4 rows of slip, to and fro, in each of the stitches of the last row. The rows touch, and therefore encircle the leaf.

3rd leaf—16 chain, skip 1, 2 slip, 1 chain, 1 double crochet on the 3rd chain, 1 chain, 1 double crochet on the 3rd chain, 1 chain, 1 double crochet on the 3rd chain, 1 slip on each of the remaining stitches, 4 rows of slip, to and fro round the leaf; 3 slip on the stitch at the top of the leaf and 3 on the one at the bottom.

When these 3 leaves are finished, join them together on the wrong side so that the end of the 2nd leaf is parallel with the last double crochet of the 1st leaf, and the end of the 3rd leaf parallel with the 1st of the last slip stitches of the 2nd leaf. Having sewn these 3 leaves together, carry on the slip stitches with the thread of the 3rd little leaf over the two others. Fasten off the thread, join it on again at the 10th slip stitch of the 3rd little leaf, counting the stitches downward from the top = 40 chain, 1 single on the 34th chain = on the ring: 10 slip, 1 slip each chain and 1 slip on each stitch of the leaves = then, make 3 more rows of slip and 2 slip on every second stitch of the 10 stitches in the ring.

Having reached the chain stitches, fasten on the thread, turn the work and continue the other rows. When the rows of slip stitches are finished, draw a thread through the chain stitches and pull them gently together.

Branch on the left and 1st leaf—22 chain, skip 1, 3 slip, 2 chain, 1 double crochet on the 2nd chain, 2 chain, 1 double crochet 1½ double crochet long, 2 chain, skip 1, 1 double crochet, 1½ double crochet long, 2 chain, skip 1, 1 treble, 2 chain, skip 1, 1 treble, 2 chain, skip 1, 1 slip on each of the remaining stitches. The remainder the same as for the right leaf.

2nd leaf—16 chain, skip 1, 2 slip, 2 chain, 1 treble, 2 chain, skip 1, 1 treble, 2 chain, skip 1, 1 treble, 2 chain, skip 1, 1 treble, 2 chain, skip 1, 1 slip on each of the remaining stitches. The rest the same as for the right leaf.

3rd leaf—12 chain, skip 1, 2 slip, 2 chain, skip 1, 1 treble, 2 chain, skip 1, 1 treble, 2 chain, skip 1, 1 treble, 2 chain, skip 1, 1 slip on each of the remaining stitches. The remainder, as well as the little ring, the same as for the right leaf. Make altogether 4 leaves for the right side and 4 for the left.

Calyx of the small flowers—11 chain = turn the work = 1 slip on the first 5 chain, 3 slip on the 6th chain, 1 slip on the 5 other chain = turn the work = * 2 chain, 1 double crochet on the 1st slip, 1 chain, 1 treble, 1 chain, 1 treble, 1 chain, ** 3 double crochets on the second of the 3 slip, on the 6th chain, repeat once from ** to * = turn the work = 1 slip on each of the preceding stitches, 3 single on the added stitch = turn the work = 1 single on the first 2 slip; slip stitches as far as the middle stitch; 13 chain, skip 1, 1 slip on each chain stitch, 6 slip, 2 single. Fasten off. Make 8 calices in all.

Small flowers of three different sizes—Make altogether, 24 large, 12 of medium size, and 16 small.

For the large flowers—18 chain, close the ring, 24 slip on the 18 chain; 1 slip on every stitch of the preceding row and 1 picot after every second slip stitch. Join the first and the last picots of 2 large flowers to the calyx, the 2nd and the 3rd picots of one large flower to the 10th and 11th picots of the other. Join the 1st and 11th picots of the 3rd flower to the 8th picot of the first and to the 5th of the second flower.

For the medium-sized flowers—14 chain, close the ring = 20 slip on the ring, then a second row of slip with 1 picot after every second slip stitch.

These flowers connect the center figure with the corner one.

For the small flowers—10 chain, close the ring = 16 slip on the ring, then a second row of slip stitches with a picot after every second stitch. Sew the medium-sized flowers and the small ones to the big ones with overcasting stitches.

The bars of chain stitches that complete the pattern they can easily be copied from the illustration.

Footnotes

[A] See at the end of the concluding chapter, the table of numbers and sizes and the list of colors of the DMC threads and cottons.

Ornament after Holbein.

Practical directions

So far, we have focused on descriptions and explanations of the different kinds of needlework. To render these complete, we must give a few practical directions regarding copying, adjustment, and transposition of the patterns, as well as to the different processes, often so essential to the ultimate success of a piece of needlework. This success does not only depend on the stitches but largely on the proper adaptation of the design to the space it is intended to fill.

Then, in the case of new lace, it is necessary to know the amount of dressing required to give it the right stiffness and, when this dressing has worn off, how to renew it. In the case of appliqué work, it is indispensable to know the ingredients paste should be composed and how to make and lay it on the work in the proper manner.

Tracing patterns against a window-pane.—In order to copy a pattern in this way, the first step is to tack or pin the piece of material or paper on the pattern to be copied. In the case of a small pattern, the tacking or pinning may be dispensed with and the two sheets held firmly pressed against the window pane with the left hand while the right hand does the tracing. Even then, it is safer to pin or gum the four corners of the two sheets together, in case of interruption, because it is difficult to fit them together again exactly.

The tracing may be done with a pencil, or better still, with a brush dipped in Indian ink or watercolor paint.

The process of tracing is easy enough, so long as the hand does not get tired, but because this generally happens very soon, it is best, if the pattern is large and complicated, to stick the sheets to the pane with strong gum or suspend them on a string, fastened across the pane by pins stuck into the window frame on either side.

To take off a pattern by rubbing.—If you want to take a pattern of a piece of embroidery direct from the work itself, lay it, right side up, flat upon a board or table and cover it with letter or tissue paper.

The paper should be of a good medium thickness. If it is too thick, it will not take a clear impression of the pattern, and if it is very thin, it is apt to tear.

Fasten the paper down upon the embroidery with pins and rub off the pattern with a crayon. Instead of a crayon, the bowl or handle of a spoon or a large silver coin will serve the purpose equally well, as will also some powdered graphite or charcoal. The outlines will not of course, in any case, be very clearly defined on the paper and will have to be gone over and carefully supplemented afterward with a pencil.

Taking off the pattern with charcoal or graphite is less injurious to the embroidery than rubbing it off with wax or metal, as the pressure required in the latter case flattens the needlework considerably. As soon as you have fixed the lines of the pattern by drawing over them with ink, it is ready for use.

To transfer a pattern directly on to the material.—Patterns cannot be copied by either of the above methods directly on to the material and can only be used when the material on which is transparent. In the case of thick close fabrics, the drawing must be made on the material itself. The following is the simplest way of transferring a pattern on to a transparent material. Begin by going over all the lines of the drawing with Indian ink so as to make them quite thick and distinct, and tacking the paper with large stitches on to the back of the material. Then mix some very dark powdered indigo diluted with water in a glass with a small pinch of sugar and powdered gum arabic, and using this as ink and a fine pen very slightly split, trace the pattern that shines through on the material.

The tracing must be very slight, for if the embroidery is not done until sometime afterward, when the lines get so firmly fixed in the material that one washing will not obliterate them; the tracing ink moreover makes the work unpleasantly sticky.

To copy with oiled paper.—Another rather expeditious mode of transferring patterns on to thin and more especially smooth glossy materials is by means of a special kind of tinted paper, called autographic paper, which is impregnated with a colored oily substance and can be found at any stationery shop. This you place between the pattern and the material, having previously fastened the material perfectly straight to a board by the line of the thread with pins. When you have fitted the two papers likewise together, go over all the lines of the pattern with a blunt pencil, or with the point of a bone crochet needle or the edge of a folder. Be careful not to press so heavily upon the pattern paper as to tear it. The pressure on the two sheets of paper, the oily substance of the blue paper discharges itself on to the material, so that when it is removed, all the lines you have traced are imprinted upon the material.

This blue tracing paper is however only available for the reproduction of patterns on washable materials, since satin and all other silky textures are discolored by it.

To pounce patterns upon materials. —The modes of copying so far described cannot be indiscriminately used for all kinds of material; cloth, velvet, and plush, for instance, are not available and pouncing is the only way that works.

The patterns, after having been transferred to straw or parchment paper, have to be pricked through. To do this, lay the paper upon cloth or felt and prick out all the lines of the drawing, making the holes, which should be clear and round, all exactly the same distance apart.

The closer and more complicated the pattern is, the finer and closer the holes should be. Every line of the outline must be carefully pricked out.

If the paper is sufficiently thin, several pouncings can be pricked at the same time, and a symmetrical design can be folded together into four and all pricked at once.

Next, the pricked pattern has to be tacked upon the material, the side from which the pricking was done next to the material and the little funnel-shaped holes on top. Paper and material must be firmly fastened down and kept in position by pins, so that neither of them will move during the process. Otherwise, you will have double lines on the material, which you will find very confusing afterward.

For pouncing, use either powdered chalk or charcoal, depending on how dark or light the material is. Dip the pouncing implement, a thing like a small drumstick materialed and covered with cloth into the powder and rub it lightly over the whole surface of the pricked pattern, so that the powder penetrates through the pinholes to the material. Instead of a proper pouncing implement, you can take a small strip of cloth, roll it around a stick, wind a string around it, and dip this into the powder.

When the powder has penetrated to the material, remove the paper, and if the pattern is to be repeated, lay it on again further on, taking care to make the lines meet exactly so that the join may not be seen.

When you have finished the pouncing and taken off the paper, proceed to draw or paint in the pattern with watercolor paints. Ackermann's are the best for the purpose. No others, as far as our experience has proved, adhere so well to even the roughest fabrics or so little affect the brilliancy of the embroidery thread. Four paints, blue, black, yellow, and white are sufficient for all purposes, whatever the color of the material may be.

The tracing may be done with a pen on a smooth surface, but a small sable-hair brush is preferable under all circumstances.

The rougher and more hairy the surface, the finer the brush ought to be, in order that the color may sink well in between the fibers.

Before beginning to paint in the pattern, gently blow away all the superfluous powder from the surface. This process may be objected to as being an old one superseded by new inventions. A resinous powder for instance, can be fixed, as soon as they have been pounced, by passing a hot iron over the material, a sheet of paper having first been laid upon it to protect it. A mixture of gum and powder can also be dissolved on the material itself by the steam of spirits-of-wine, and various other processes needless to mention here can be used. Some are only useful in tracing patterns on a large scale, while others require a variety of appliances, not as a rule, within the reach of those to whom needlework is a simple recreation.

The preparation of the materials and the subdivision of the patterns.—Long years of experience and practice have brought us in contact with a many designers, many of them artists in their way, so long as it was only a question of putting their own compositions on paper but who yet found themselves confronted by real difficulties the moment they were called upon to transfer them to material.

We shall, as much as possible, point out to our readers the precautions to be taken in tracing patterns and must for that purpose go back to one of the first operations, namely that of pricking.

To begin, the paper on which the pattern is should always be large enough for there to be a clear margin of 4 to 5 cm (1½ to 2 in.) all around the pattern, so that the pouncing instrument may never come in contact with the material beneath.

In transferring patterns to material, no lines of division should ever be made directly upon it with lead, chalk, or charcoal, as it is hardly ever possible entirely to remove them, and they often become very confusing afterward.

Before beginning the tracing, divide your material into four, then decide what the width of the border outside the pattern is to be. It is quite an exceptional thing to carry a pattern right up to the edge. Materials that will bend, such as all linen and cotton textures, can be folded in four. Like the paper, the folds must be pinched and pressed down so that the lines may remain clear and distinct until the tracing be finished.

After dividing it into four, mark out the diagonal lines. These are absolutely necessary in order to get the corner figures rightly placed.

Though most of our readers know how to make these lines on paper with a pencil and ruler, few, easy as it is, know how to make them upon material. You have only to fold over the corner of your piece of material so that the outside thread of the warp or cut edge run parallel with the woof edge, which marks the angle of the fold-over.

This double folding over divides the ground into 8 parts. Arranging for the outside border or margin is easy enough if the material and the kind of work you are going to do upon it allowing for the drawing out of threads, since then a thread drawn out each way serves as a guide for tracing the pattern, straight to the line of the material. It is often better, however, not to draw out the threads for an open-work border until the pattern is traced. If you do not wish to or are not able to draw out threads to mark the pattern and you are working on a material of which the threads can be counted, follow the directions explained in fig. 252.

You cannot mark cloth, silk materials, or plush by folding them in the above way, cloth, and some kinds of silken textures will not take a bend, and others that will would be spoiled by it.

All such materials should be mounted in a frame, before the pattern is traced, and the ground be then divided out in the following way: take a strong thread, make a knot at one end, stick a pin into it, and tighten the knot round it. With a pair of compasses, divide one of the sides into two equal parts, stick the pin with the knot around it in at the middle and the same on the opposite side, putting in a second pin to stretch the thread. Carry other threads across in a similar way, in the width of the material and from corner to corner, and you will have your ground correctly marked out, in such a manner as to leave no marks when, after pouncing in the pattern, you remove the threads. Before finishing the pouncing of a pattern, see that it is the right size for the purpose it is intended for.

Supposing that you are tracing a border with a corner, measure the length it will occupy and then by a very light pouncing, you can mark the points from which the pattern will have to be repeated. It may be that a gap will be left in the middle, which, if not too large, can be eliminated without altering the pattern by pushing the whole thing a little further in and so shortening the distance between the two corners.

Should the gap be too large for this, you will have to make a supplementary design to fill up the place. The same thing would be necessary in the case of your having to shorten a pattern.

Figure 885

To transpose and repeat patterns by means of looking-glasses (Fig. 885).—We have referred to the necessity that often occurs of adapting patterns to certain given proportions; this can in most cases be done easily enough without the help of a draughtsman, especially in the case of cross-stitch embroideries, by means of two unframed looking-glasses (Penelope mirrors, as they are called) used in the following manner.

If you want to utilize only a piece of a straight border, or after repeating it several times, to form a corner with it, place the mirror in the first instance across it at right angles, at the place from which the pattern is to be repeated, and then exactly diagonally inward.

To make a square out of a straight pattern, take two mirrors and place them such that they touch at the point where the diagonal lines meet, as represented in fig. 885, and you have your square at once.

This is all easy enough, but before beginning any large piece of work it is necessary to consider carefully which parts of the drawing will best fill the center and which are best suited to form the corners, as it is not every part of a straight pattern that is adapted for repetition.

A few preliminary trials with the help of the mirrors will better show the importance of these explanations than anything further we can say on the subject.

Figure 886

To alter the proportions of a pattern by dividing the ground into squares (Figs. 886 and 887).—Cases will occur where it will be found necessary to subject the pattern to greater modifications still than those we have been dealing with so far.

You want, for example, to embroider a rather large running ground pattern on a piece of material that is relatively too small for the subject or a small and rather minute pattern on a large surface, on which it is likely to look either too insignificant, or too crowded and confused. Chances are, if you do not know how to draw, you will either think it necessary to get a draughtsman to help you or you will give up the piece of work altogether, deterred by the difficulties that confront you. You need not do either if you will follow the directions here given.

Take a sheet of large-sized quadrille paper, which, if necessary, you can prepare for yourself and trace your pattern upon it, or rule the squares direct upon the drawing, as shown in fig. 886.

On a second sheet of vegetable paper, rule squares, a fourth, a third or half as small again as those on the first sheet. Thus, if the sides of the first squares be 15 mm (.6 in.) long and you want to reduce your pattern by one fifth, the sides of your new squares should measure only 12 mm (about ½ in.).

If, on the contrary, you want to enlarge the pattern by one-fifth, make

Figure 887

the sides of your squares 18 mm (.7 in.) long.

Then follow, square by square, the lines of the drawing, extending or contracting them according to whether the pattern is to be enlarged or diminished.

To copy a pattern directly from a piece of embroidery and enlarge or diminish it at the same time, proceed as follows: fix the embroidery on a board, stretching it equally in every direction; then measure the length of the drawing, divide the centimeters by the number of units corresponding to whatever the proportions of your copy are to be, and if there are any fractions of centimeters over, subdivide them into millimeters, if necessary, into half millimeters and make your division by whatever measure you have adopted. Take a pair of compasses with dry points, open them sufficiently for the opening to correspond to the number and the distance obtained by the division, then plant a pin with a thread fastened to it, at the point indicated by the point of the compasses and repeat the last operation all along one side of the embroidery and, if possible, a little beyond it, so that it may not be defaced by the marks of the pins. All you have to do now is pull the threads in perfectly straight lines to the opposite side and carry other threads across them in a similar manner so that the whole surface be divided into squares.

It is needless to say that if you have to trace a pattern from a mounted piece of work, you cannot stretch it on a board. With a little invention, however, some way pins can be so as not to injure the work.

To alter the width of a pattern retaining the original height (Figs. 888, 889, 890).—Sometimes it is necessary to lengthen out a pattern without altering its height. In this case, you modify the shape of the square

Figure 888

Figure 889

Figure 890

and make long or narrow squares, according to the general shape of the design you wish to reproduce. Fig. 888 represents a pattern in Soutache DMC, marked out in squares; in fig. 889 the squares are lengthened out a third beyond their original size and the pattern is expanded; in fig. 890, the squares are compressed to a third less than their original size.

This method of subdividing patterns greatly facilitates the alterations they have so often to undergo, and we are sure that few among those who have any real aptitude for needlework cannot draw enough to be able to copy the contents of a square.

Fig. 888. Pattern in soutache. Original size.

Fig. 889. Pattern in fig. 888 drawn out in the width.

Fig. 890. Pattern in fig. 888 compressed in the width.

To prepare the paste for appliqué work.—It may seem strange to devote a separate paragraph to such an apparently simple operation; but in appliqué work it is most important, as not only the material on which the work is done but all the expensive accessories are liable to be spoiled by paste that has been badly prepared.

Put some wheat (not rice) starch into a vessel with a rounded bottom, add just enough water to dissolve the starch, and stir the substance with a wooden spoon until it becomes perfectly smooth.

In the meantime, put about ¼ of a pint (½ cup) of clean water on the fire (high heat) to boil, and when it boils, add a little powdered pitch or carpenter's glue, about the size of a pea, and pour in the starch, stirring it the whole time. When the mixture has boiled up several times, take it off the heat and go on stirring it till it gets cold, otherwise lumps will form in it, which we pointed out in the preceding chapter, must never be allowed to get in between the material and the paper.

This kind of paste makes no spots and does not injure even the most delicate colors since it does not contain acid. In winter, it will keep for several days, but in hot weather, it very soon begins to ferment and should then on no account be used.

Gum arabic ought never to be used for appliqué work, as it becomes so hard that it is impossible to get the needle through, and the saccharine it contains almost always causes ugly spots to appear in the material when it dries.

When the work is finished, it is a good plan to spread a very thin layer of paste over the entire back of it with a fine brush made of hog's bristles, and not to take it out of the frame until it is perfectly dry.

To stiffen new needlework.—In the chapter on Irish lace, page 68, we said that new needlework of that kind had to be ironed. This should be done in the following manner: when the lace has been taken off its foundation, lay it facedown on a piece of fine white flannel; then dip a piece of very stiff new organdy muslin into water, take it out again almost immediately and wring it slightly, so that no drops may fall from it, and then dab the wrong side of the lace all over with this pad of damp muslin and iron it with a hot iron, which should be moved slowly forward so that the moisture which the organdy has imparted to the lace may evaporate slowly. Not until you are quite sure that the lace is dry should it be taken off the board.

There is no better way than this of giving new lace that almost imperceptible degree of stiffness by which alone it is often to be distinguished from old. Water only does not stiffen the thread sufficiently and it is difficult with starch to hit upon exactly the right consistency, whereas the organdy muslin supplies just the right amount.

Embroidered network can be stiffened in the same manner and should be damped in the frame on the wrong side and not taken off until it is quite dry.

We even recommend embroidery on linen being treated in the same way, except that when the linen is very creased, cover it with a damp cloth and iron upon that first, then take the cloth away and iron the embroidery itself so as to dry it completely.

To wash ordinary lace.—Wind it around a bottle the same width top and bottom and cover it entirely with muslin, fastened to the lace by a few stitches. Fill the bottle halfway with sand so will not get knocked about too violently when the water boils.

Immerse the bottle in a saucepan of cold water with a piece of soap the size of a nut in it, and if the lace is dirty, a small pinch of salt, and let it boil for about an hour, pouring off the water as it gets dirty and adding clean.

When all the dirt has been boiled out of the lace, which you will know to be the case when the water remains perfectly clear, rinse out the soap before taking the lace off the bottle, by plunging it into cold water.

To wash real lace.—The process is the same as the above, but since real lace is so seldom washed and is generally very yellow and fragile, particularly if it has been roughly used, it is rather difficult to clean.

If stained or greasy, the lace should be left to soak in good olive oil for several hours or even days. This restores to the thread that softness and smoothness which use and bad washing had impaired. After the oil bath, the lace should be washed on a bottle in the manner already described.

To stiffen lace.—Dip the lace when perfectly dry in thin starch prepared as follows.

Take as much fine wheat starch as you think you will require, divide it into two portions and dissolve both in cold water. Boil the one portion, and when it has cooled enough to have stopped steaming, stir the cold starch into it and dilute the whole with cold water to the consistency of thick cream. If the lace is to be slightly colored, add a few drops of black coffee, or dilute the starch with weak tea or guimauve water; the coffee will give it a dark cream color, either of the latter a pale greenish hue.

Dip the lace in the mixture and squeeze it out gently without wringing it to get rid of all the superfluous liquid, then lay it flat on the left hand and beat it for a few minutes with the right to work the starch well in; repeat the whole process twice, then roll the lace in fine linen and leave it there until you are ready to iron or pin it out, as the case may be.

To iron lace.—After the lace has lain for an hour or two in the cloth, iron it if it be machine-made and if it be Irish Guipure or real point lace of any sort, pin it out.

Before you begin to iron, hold the lace tight in your left hand by the footing, and with the right hand, pull out all the picots, along the edge of the lace, to an equal length, then lay it out flat upon a board covered with white flannel and iron it with a moderately hot iron, passing the iron backward and forward over it until it is quite dry.

If creases should come in the ironing where they ought not to be, dab them over lightly with a sponge moistened with water and a few drops of starch and pass the iron over them again.

After ironing the whole length of lace, pull it out crossways from left to right, and from right to left, and iron it all over once more. This does away with the artificial stiffness and gives it the agreeable softness and pliancy of new lace.

To pin out lace.—In order to pin out lace in a thoroughly satisfactory manner, you should provide yourself with a wooden drum, about 30 cm (12 in.). high and from 50 to 60 cm (20 to 22 in.) in diameter, large enough to rest upon the knees.

The outside circumference of the wood should be padded and covered with grey or white ticking.

The pins must be exactly the size of the picots they are to pin down; you will require extremely fine ones for Valenciennes and coarser for other kinds of lace. Steel pins are of no use whatever, because of their liability to rust. Cover the cylinder with blue paper (less trying for the eyes than any other) and take only just as much lace out of the damp cloth as you are likely to be able to pin out before it gets dry, keeping the remainder covered up.

Lay the lace upon the drum and pin the footing down first in a straight line, sticking the pins in pretty closely and at regular distances apart; then pin down each picot separately, taking care not to open them if they have kept their original shape and to shut them up by twisting them if they have got untwisted.

If you find the pinning out troublesome and cannot get it all done before the lace dries, dampen the picots with a sponge as you proceed.

Lace should never be pinned out when it is dry as the threads of the picots are then very apt to break and torn picots destroy the value of even the best lace.

Raised lace has to be stamped out from the wrong side with a lace awl or kind of pricker of bone made for the purpose. Some professional lace-cleaners use this implement even for Valenciennes lace but we cannot recommend it, seeing that it is a lace that is by nature perfectly flat.

Let the length of lace you have pinned out remain on the drum until it is quite dry. If you have several yards to pin out, wind it around and around the cylinder. Cover up the lace as you proceed and put each length away as soon as it is ready in a blue

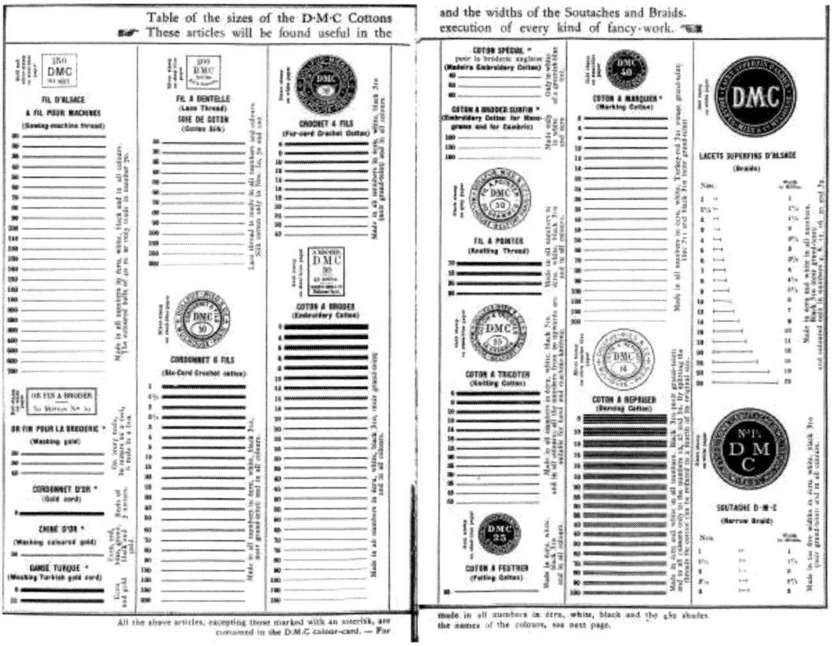

paper bag, so as to keep the whole perfectly clean.

In conclusion, we may remark that the cleaning of lace should only be undertaken when you are fairly sure of not being interrupted, because more especially the pinning requires to be finished off as quickly as possible.

To wash colored cottons and work done with the same.—In order to test the fastness of the dyes, untie the skeins and pour boiling water over them, leave them to soak for about fifteen minutes, soap and rub them lightly from end to end, and rinse them out thoroughly in as many changes of cold water as may be found necessary, until the water remains perfectly colorless.

Squeeze out all the water you can and let the cottons dry quickly without exposing them to the sun.

Colored cottons are often washed in vinegar, because it is supposed to affect the color less than water does. We have come to the conclusion after several trials that this is a delusion, for the good dyes keep their color without the aid of vinegar and the bad ones wash out in spite of it.

The fast colors lose none of their beauty in the process, nor does it affect the quality of the cotton; any excess of coloring matter which the fibers of the cotton may have absorbed in the process of dyeing is got rid of this way.

If a piece of work has been done with unwashed cottons and the colors run in the first washing, you have only to rinse it out in several changes of tepid water to restore it to its original freshness, and if you want to give it a yellowish tinge, it should be dipped it in weak tea or coffee.

Materials: It was stated in the preface that our readers would find the choice of colors and material rendered comparatively easy to them by the notes affixed to the illustrations, but these notes, in spite of all the care bestowed upon them must still have remained very incomplete had it not been for the following tables which we were fortunately able to append to our work and which will help everyone to choose their own materials without having them actually before them. The strokes that are affixed to each number indicate the exact size of the thread, so to find out the number you want to buy, you have but to lay your pattern thread, stretching it slightly, on the strokes, in succession, till you come to the one that matches it in size.

With regard to the colors, the names and shades of which have been classed in the second table with the greatest care, and of which our workers have no less than 460 to choose from [3], all those referred to in connection with our illustrations are quite fast dyes [4], save in a few instances in which we were forced to make an exception in favor of a doubtful color to secure a harmonious effect.

A complete table of colors must include certain more or less staring shades, which though they may not be to every one's taste, cannot on that account be left out.

We conclude our work with the well-meant and by no means useless recommendation to our readers: never to begin a piece of work of any considerable size without first making sure that the colors they intend to use are fast and providing themselves with a larger supply of materials than even on a close calculation they think they are likely to require, lest they should find themselves having either to leave their work unfinished or finish it with materials that do not match. There is generally a slight difference in tone between cottons that have been bought at different times, and there is also a reasonable likelihood, considering their great variety, of some mistake being made in the number by either buyer or seller in ordering a fresh supply.

All of the above articles, excepting those marked with an asterisk, are made in all numbers in écru, white, black and the 450 shades contained in the DMC color card.

—For the names of the colors, see next page.

Alphabetical list of the names and the numbers of the 450 shades DMC Alsace Thread, Sewing and Embroidery Cottons, contained in the DMC color-card, in any of which shades the knitting Cotton, Soutaches and Braids etc. are to be had.					
Couleurs Colors	**Très-foncé** Very dark	**Foncé** Dark	**Moyen** Medium	**Clair** Light	**Très-clair** Very light
Bleu d'Azur	...	3325	...	...	...
Bleu-Canard	3395	3306	3307	3308	3309
Bleu cendré	...	...	448	...	...
Bleu de Ciel	515	516	517	518	519
Bleu-Fayence	481	482	483	484	485
Bleu de France	337	338	339	340	341
Bleu-Gentiane	476	477	478	479	480
Bleu-Gris	3300	3301	3302	3303	3304
Bleu-Indigo	336	311	312	322	334
Bleu-Lapis	342	333	343	344	345
Bleu-Marin	505	506	507	508	509
Bleu-Outremer	...	682	683	...	...
Bleu pâle	...	...	...	668	...
Bleu-Prunelle	486	487	488	489	490
Bleu tendre	...	...	...	...	709
Bleu vert	525	526	527	528	529
Bleu violacé	...	674	675	...	...
——					
Bronze doré	585	586	587	588	589
——					
Brun-Acajou	300	400	301	401	402
Brun-Cachou	433	434	435	436	437
Brun-Cannelle	660	661	662	663	664
Brun-Caroubier	354	355	303	356	357
Brun-Chamois	416	417	324	418	419
Brun-Cuir	430	431	302	432	325
Brun-Feuille-morte	615	616	617	618	619
Brun-Havane	454	455	456	457	458
Brun-Loutre	438	439	440	441	442
Brun-Marron	403	404	405	406	407
Brun-Myrthe	...	...	463	...	...
Brun-Puce	459	...	...	...	...
Brun-Rouille	3310	3311	3312	3313	3314
——					

Gris-Acier	650	651	652	653	654
Gris-Amadou	329	383	384	385	386
Gris d'Argent	...	...	719	...	...
Gris-Bleu	590	591	592	593	594
Gris-Bois	610	611	612	613	614
Gris-Brun	408	409	410	411	412
Gris-Castor	645	646	647	648	649
Gris-Cendre	413	317	414	318	415
Gris-Coutil	387	388	323	389	390
Gris-Deuil	655	656	657	658	659
Gris-Écru	...	704	705	706	...
Gris-Etoupe	...	707	708	...	...
Gris de Fer	600	601	602	603	604
Gris-Feutre	635	636	637	638	639
Gris-Ficelle	...	460	461	462	...
Gris-Foin	520	521	522	523	524
Gris-Fumée	640	641	642	643	644
Gris-Lin	...	...	716	717	...
Gris-Mastic	...	...	718	...	...
Gris neutre	620	621	622	623	624
Gris-Noisette	420	421	422	423	424
Gris-Perle	625	626	627	628	629
Gris de Plomb	378	379	380	381	382
Gris-Poussière	630	631	632	633	634
Gris-Souris	425	426	427	428	429
Gris-Tilleul	391	392	393	330	331
Gris verdâtre	595	596	597	598	599
——					
Jaune-Citron	...	307	445	446	...
Jaune-Crême	...	...	711	712	...
Jaune-Maïs	575	576	577	678	579
Jaune d'Ocre	...	...	676	677	...
Jaune-Orange	...	...	443	444	...
Jaune-Rouille	363	364	308	365	366
Jaune d'Or	...	...	667	...	...
Jaune-vieil-Or	678	679	680	...	...
——					
Lilas gris	313	398	314	328	399
——					
Noir grand-teint	310	...	...	...	...
Noir-Jais	681	...	...	...	...

Noir vert	473	...	...	...	...
——					
Rose-Eglantine	570	571	572	573	574
Rose tendre	...	...	...	...	3326
Rose vif	565	566	567	568	569
——					
Rouge-Aurore	360	306	361	332	362
Rouge-Bordeaux	496	497	...	...	...
Rouge-Cardinal	346	347	304	305	348
Rouge-Cerise	3315	3316	3317	3318	3319
Rouge-Corinthe	...	...	447	...	...
Rouge-Cornouille	...	449	450	...	...
Rouge-Ecarlate	...	498	464	...	...
Rouge-Framboise	684	685	686	687	688
Rouge-Géranium	349	350	351	352	353
Rouge-Grenat	358	359	326	309	335
Rouge-Groseille	605	606	607	608	609
Rouge-Maroquin	...	...	3327	3328	3329
Rouge-Turc	...	...	321	...	...
Rouge-Vermillon	...	...	666	...	...
——					
Vert-Bouteille	491	492	493	494	495
Vert-Bronze	669	670	671	672	673
Vert-Canard	545	546	547	548	549
Vert-Corbeau	665	...	...	...	...
Vert doré	580	581	582	583	584
Vert d'Eau	...	...	713	714	715
Vert-de-gris	...	474	475	...	...
Vert-Emeraude	555	556	557	558	559
Vert-Fauve	689	690	691	692	693
Vert-Lierre	500	501	502	503	504
Vert-Madeira	...	...	...	710	...
Vert-Malachite	560	561	562	563	564
Vert métallique	465	466	467	...	...
Vert-Mousse	468	469	470	471	472
Vert-Myrthe	535	536	537	538	539
Vert-Olive	510	511	512	513	514
Vert-Perroquet	694	695	696	697	698
Vert-Pistache	319	367	320	368	369
Vert-Pré	699	700	701	702	703
Vert russe	...	499	...	...	...

——					
Violet-Améthyste	3320	3321	3322	3323	3324
Violet-Evêque	451	452	453	...	...
Violet-Lie-de-vin	370	371	372	373	374
Violet-Mauve	375	315	376	316	377
Violet-de-Parme	540	541	542	543	544
Violet-Pensée	530	531	532	533	534
Violet-Prune	550	551	552	553	554
Violet-Scabieuse	394	327	395	396	397
Couleurs Colors	**Très-foncé** Very dark	**Foncé** Dark	**Moyen** Medium	**Clair** Light	**Très-clair** Very light

To avoid mistakes the public is urgently requested to designate the colors by the number, never by name.

The colors whose numbers begin with 3 or 4 are the fastest.

Further information respecting mode of execution, materials and so forth may be had by applying to the firm of

TH. de DILLMONT, DORNACH (Alsace).

FOOTNOTES:

[3] The DMC color-card consists of 450 shades about half of which are fast dyes. See the list of names on pp. 572 and 573.

[4] By fast (bon-teint) colors are meant those which will bear ordinary and repeated washing. There are only very few which are really fast, or grand-teint, that is to say, which will resist the action of chemical agents, amongst of these, the black, Noir 310, is quite indestructible.

About the Author

Thérèse Maria Joseph de Dillmont was born in 1846 and studied in Vienna at an embroidery school founded by the Empress Marie-Therese. After completing her schooling, she moved to Donarch, a village near Mulhouse, France, and founded her own embroidery school at a time when most aristocratic woman confined their embroidery to salons and boudoirs. The success of Dillmont's school in Mulhouse led to shops bearing her name in Vienna, Paris, London, and Berlin. A true pioneer of needlework, she traveled extensively, studied needlework in many countries, and collected hundreds of pieces of outstanding embroidery.

0 26575 11862 9